MOZART

THE MAN AND THE ARTIST
REVEALED IN HIS OWN WORDS

MOZART

THE MAN AND THE ARTIST
REVEALED IN HIS OWN WORDS

Compiled and Annotated by
FRIEDRICH KERST

Translated into English, and Edited,
with Additional Notes, by
HENRY EDWARD KREHBIEL

DOVER PUBLICATIONS, INC.
NEW YORK

This Dover edition, first published in 1965, is
an unabridged and unaltered republication of the
work first published by Geoffrey Bles, London,
in 1926.

International Standard Book Number: 0-486-21316-1

Library of Congress Catalog Card Number 64-18855

Manufactured in the United States of America

Dover Publications, Inc.
180 Varick Street
New York 14, N.Y.

EDITOR'S NOTE

The purpose and scope of this little book will be obvious to the reader from even a cursory glance at its contents. It is, in a way, an autobiography of Mozart written without conscious purpose, and for that reason peculiarly winning, illuminating and convincing. The outward things in Mozart's life are all but ignored in it, but there is a frank and full disclosure of the great musician's aristic, intellectual and moral character, made in his own words.

The Editor has not only taken the trouble to revise the work of the German author and compiler, but, for reasons which seemed to him imperative has also made a new translation of all the excerpts. Most of the translations of Mozart's letters which have found their way into the books betray want of familiarity with the idioms and colloquialisms employed by Mozart, as well as understanding of his careless, contradictory and sprawling epistolary style. Some of the intimacy of that style the new translation seeks to preserve, but the purpose has chiefly been to make the meaning plain.

H. E. K.

New York, June 7, 1905

CONTENTS

MOZART

THE MAN AND THE ARTIST
REVEALED IN HIS OWN WORDS

THE SIGNIFICANCE OF
MOZART

Mozart! What a radiance streams from the name! Bright and pure as the light of the sun, Mozart's music greets us. We pronounce his name and behold! the youthful artist is before us,—the merry, light-hearted smile upon his features, which belongs only to true and naïve genius. It is impossible to imagine an aged Mozart,—an embittered and saddened Mozart,—glowering gloomily at a wicked world which is doing its best to make his lot still more burdensome;—a Mozart whose music should reflect such painful moods.

Mozart was a Child of the Sun. Filled with a humor truly divine, he strolled unconstrainedly through a multitude of cares like *Prince Tamino* through his fantastic trials. Music was his talisman, his magic flute with which he could exorcise all the petty terrors that beset him. Has such a man and artist—one who was completely resolved in his works, and therefore still stands bodily before us with all his glorious qualities after the lapse of a century—has Mozart still something to say to us who have just stepped timidly into a new century separated by another from that of the composer? Much; very much. Many prophets have arisen since Mozart's death; two of them have moved us profoundly with their evangel. One of them knew all the mysteries, and Nature took away his hearing lest he proclaim too much. We followed him into all the depths of the world of feeling. The other shook us awake and placed us in the hurly-burly of national life and striving; pointing to his own achievements, he said: "If you wish it, you have now a German art!" The one was Beethoven,—the other Wagner. Because their music demands of

1

us that we share with it its experiences and struggles, they are the guiding spirits of a generation which has grown up in combat and is expecting an unknown world of combat beyond the morning mist of the new century.

But we are in the case of the man in the fairy tale who could not forget the merry tune of the forest bird which he had heard as a boy. We gladly permit ourselves to be led, occasionally, out of the rude realities that surround us, into a beautiful world that knows no care but lies forever bathed in the sunshine of cloudless happiness,—a world in which every loveliness of which fancy has dreamed has taken life and form. It is because of this that we make pilgrimages to the masterpieces of the plastic arts, that we give heed to the speech of Schiller, listen to the music of Mozart. When wearied by the stress of life we gladly hie to Mozart that he may tell us stories of that land of beauty, and convince us that there are other and better occupations than the worries and combats of the fleeting hour. This is what Mozart has to tell us to-day. In spite of Wagner he has an individual mission to fulfill which will keep him immortal. "That of which Lessing convinces us only with expenditure of many words sounds clear and irresistible in 'The Magic Flute':—the longing for light and day. Therefore there is something like the glory of daybreak in the tones of Mozart's opera; it is wafted towards us like the morning breeze which dispels the shadows and invokes the sun."

Mozart remains ever young; one reason is because death laid hold of him in the middle of his career. While all the world was still gazing expectantly upon him, he vanished from the earth and left no hope deceived. His was the enviable fate of a Raphael, Schiller and Körner. As the German ('tis Schumann's utterance) thinks of Beethoven when he speaks the word symphony, so the name of Mozart in his mind is associated with the conception of things youthful, bright and sunny. Schumann was fully conscious of a purpose when he called out, "Do not put Beethoven in the hands of young people too early; refresh and strengthen them with the fresh and lusty Mozart." Another time he writes: "Does it not seem as if Mozart's works become fresher and fresher the oftener we hear them?"

The more we realize that Wagner places a heavy and intoxicating draught before us, the more we shall appreciate the precious mountain spring which laves us in Mozart's music, and the less willing we shall be to permit any opportunity to pass unimproved which offers us the crystal cup. In the mind of Goethe genius was summed up in the name of Mozart. In a prophetic ecstasy he spoke the significant words: "What else is genius than that productive power through which deeds arise, worthy of standing in the presence of God and Nature, and which, for this reason, bear results and are lasting? All the creations of Mozart are of this class; within them there is a generative force which is transplanted from generation to generation, and is not likely soon to be exhausted or devoured."

CHIPS FROM THE WORKSHOP

1. If one has the talent it pushes for utterance and torments one; it will out; and then one is out with it without questioning. And, look you, there is nothing in this thing of learning out of books. Here, here and here [pointing to his ear, his head and his heart] is your school. If everything is right there, then take your pen and down with it; afterward ask the opinion of a man who knows his business.

To a musically talented boy who asked Mozart how one might learn to compose.

2. I can not write poetically; I am no poet. I can not divide and subdivide my phrases so as to produce light and shade; I am no painter. I can not even give expression to my sentiments and thoughts by gestures and pantomime; I am no dancer. But I can do it with tones; I am a musician. . . . I wish you might live till there is nothing more to be said in music.

Mannheim, November 8, 1777, in a letter of congratulation to his father, who was born on November 14, 1719. Despite his assertion, Mozart was an admirable dancer and passionately devoted to the sport. [So says Herr Kerst, obviously misconceiving Mozart's words. It is plain to me that the composer had the classic definition of the dance in mind when he said that he was no dancer. The dance of which he was thinking was that described by Charles Kingsley. "A dance in which every motion was a word, and rest as eloquent as motion; in which every attitude was a fresh motive for a sculptor of the purest school, and the highest physical activity was manifested, not as in coarse pantomime, in fantastic bounds and unnatural distortions, but in perpetual delicate modulations of a stately and self-sustained grace." H. E. K.]

3. The poets almost remind me of the trumpeters with their tricks of handicraft. If we musicians were to stick as faithfully to our rules (which were very good as long as we had no better) we should make as worthless music as they make worthless books.

Vienna, October 13, 1781, to his father. He is writing about the libretto of "Die Entführung aus dem Serail," by Stephanie. The trumpeters at the time still made use of certain flourishes which had been traditionally preserved in their guild.

       .

4. I have spared neither care nor labor to produce something excellent for Prague. Moreover it is a mistake to think that the practise of my art has become easy to me. I assure you, dear friend, no one has given so much care to the study of composition as I. There is scarcely a famous master in music whose works I have not frequently and diligently studied.

A remark to Conductor Kucharz in Prague, who led the rehearsals for "Don Giovanni" in 1787.

5. They are, indeed, the fruit of long and painstaking labor; but the hope which some of my friends aroused in me, that my work would be rewarded at least in part, has given me courage and the flattering belief that these, my offspring, will some day bring me comfort.

From the dedication of the Six Quartets to Haydn in 1785. The quartets were sent back to the publisher, Artaria, from Italy, because "they contained so many misprints." The unfamiliar chords and dissonances were looked upon as printers' errors. Grassalkowitsch, a Hungarian prince, thought his musicians were playing faultily in some of these passages, and when he learned differently he tore the music in pieces.

6. I can not deny, but must confess that I shall be glad when I receive my release from this place. Giving lessons here is no fun; you must work yourself pretty tired, and if you don't give a good many lessons you will make but little money. You must not think that it is laziness;—no!—but it goes counter to my genius, counter to my mode of life. You know that, so to speak, I am wrapped up in music,—that I practise it all day long,—that I like to specu-

late, study, consider. All this is prevented by my mode of life here. I shall, of course, have some free hours, but they will be so few that they will be necessary more for recuperation than work.

Paris, July 31, 1778, to his father.

7. M. Le Gros bought the *Sinfonia concertante* of me. He thinks that he is the only one who has it; but that isn't so. It is still fresh in my head, and as soon as I get home I'll write it down again.

Paris, October 3, 1778, to his father. An evidence of the retentiveness of Mozart's memory. In this instance, however, he did not carry out his expressed intention. Le Gros was director of the *Concerts spirituels*.

8. Melody is the essence of music. I compare a good melodist to a fine racer, and counterpointists to hack post-horses; therefore be advised, let well alone and remember the old Italian proverb: *Chi sa più, meno sa*—"Who knows most, knows least."

To the English tenor Michael Kelly, about 1786, in answer to Kelly's question whether or not he should take up the study of counterpoint.

9. One of the priests gave me a theme. I took it on a promenade and in the middle [the fugue was in G minor] I began in the major, with something jocose but in the same tempo; finally the theme again, but backwards. Finally I wondered if I might not use the playful melody as a theme for a fugue. I did not question long, but made it at once, and it went as accurately as if Daser had measured it for the purpose. The dean was beside himself.

Augsburg, October 23, 1777, to his father. Daser was a tailor in Salzburg.

10. Above us is a violinist, below us another, next door a singing teacher who gives lessons, and in the last room opposite ours, a hautboyist. Merry conditions for composing! You get so many ideas!

Milan, August 23, 1771, to his "dearest sister."

11. If I but had the theme on paper,—worked out, of course. It is too silly that we have got to hatch out our work in a room.

A remark to his wife while driving through a beautiful bit of nature and humming all manner of ideas that came into his head.

12. I'd be willing to work forever and forever if I were permitted to write only such music as I want to write and can write —which I myself think good. Three weeks ago I made a symphony, and by to-morrow's post I shall write again to Hofmeister and offer him three pianoforte quartets, if he has the money.

Written in 1789 to a baron who was his friend and who had submitted a symphony for his judgment. F. A. Hofmeister was a composer and publisher in Vienna.

13. You can do a thing like this for the pianoforte, but not for the theatre. When I wrote this I was still too fond of hearing my own music, and never could make an end.

A remark to Rochlitz while revising and abbreviating the principal air in "Die Entführung."

14. You know that I had already finished the first *Allegro* on the second day after my arrival here, and consequently had seen Mademoiselle Cannabich only once. Then came young Danner and asked me how I intended to write the *Andante*. "I will make it fit the character of Mademoiselle Rose." When I played it it pleased immensely. . . . I was right; she is just like the *Andante*.

Mannheim, December 6, 1777, to his father. Rose Cannabich was a pupil of Mozart's, aged thirteen and very talented. "She is very sensible for her age, has a staid manner, is serious, speaks little, but when she does speak it is with grace and amiability," writes Mozart in the same letter. It is also related of Beethoven that he sometimes delineated persons musically. [Also Schumann. H. E. K.]

15. I have composed a Quintet for Oboe, Clarinet, Horn, Bassoon and Pianoforte, which has been received with extraordinary favor [Köchel, No. 452]. I myself think it the best thing I ever wrote in my life.

Vienna, April 10, 1784, to his father.

16. As an exercise I have set the aria, *Non so d'onde viene,* which Bach composed so beautifully. I did it because I know Bach so well, and the aria pleases me so much that I can't get it out of my head. I wanted to see whether or not in spite of these things I was able to make an aria that should not be a bit like Bach's. It isn't a bit, not a bit like it.

Mannheim, February 28, 1778, to his father. The lovely aria is No. 294 in Köchel's catalogue. The Bach referred to was Johann Christian, the "London" Bach.

17. I haven't a single quiet hour here. I can not write except at night and consequently can not get up early. One is not always in the mood for writing. Of course I could scribble all day long, but these things go out into the world and I want not to be ashamed of myself when I see my name on them. And then, as you know, I become stupid as soon as I am obliged to write for an instrument that I can not endure. Occasionally for the sake of a change I have composed something else—pianoforte duets with the violin, and a bit of the mass.

Mannheim, February 14, 1778, to his father. Mozart was ill disposed toward the pianoforte at the time. His love for Aloysia Weber occupied the most of his attention and time.

18. Herewith I am sending you a Prelude and a three-voiced Fugue [Köchel, No. 394]. . . . It is awkwardly written; the prelude must come first and the fugue follow. The reason for its appearance is because I had made the fugue and wrote it out while I was thinking out the prelude.

Vienna, April 20, 1782, to his sister Marianne. Here Mozart gives us evidence of his manner of composing; he worked out his compositions completely in his mind and was then able, even after considerable time had elapsed, to write them down, in which proceeding nothing could disturb him. In the case before us, while engaged in the more or less mechanical labor of transcription he thought out a new composition. Concerning the fugue and its origin he continues to gossip in the same letter.

19. The cause of this fugue seeing the light of this world is my dear Constanze. Baron von Swieten, to whom I go every Sunday, let me carry home all the works of Händel and Sebastian Bach after I had played them through for him. Constanze fell in love with the fugues as soon as she had heard them; she doesn't want to hear anything but fugues, especially those of Händel and Bach. Having often heard me improvise fugues she asked me if I had never written any down, and when I said no, she gave me a good scolding, for not being willing to write the most beautiful things in music, and did not cease her begging until I had composed one for her, and so it came about. I purposely wrote the indication *Andante maestoso*, so that it should not be played too rapidly;—for unless a fugue is played slowly the entrance of the subject will not be distinctly and clearly heard and the piece will be ineffective. As soon as I find time and opportunity I shall write five more.

Vienna, April 20, 1782, to his sister Marianne. Cf. No. 93. [Mozart's remark that he carried home "all the works" of Händel and Bach, must, of course, be read as meaning all that were in print at the time. H. E. K.]

20. I have no small amount of work ahead of me. By Sunday week I must have my opera arranged for military band or somebody will be ahead of me and carry away the profits; and I must also write a new symphony. How will that be possible? You have no idea how difficult it is to make such an arrangement so that it shall be adapted to wind instruments and yet lose nothing of its effect. Well, well;—I shall have to do the work at night.

Vienna, July 20, 1782, to his father who had asked for a symphony for the Hafner family in Salzburg. The opera referred to is "Die Entführung aus dem Serail."

21. I was firmly resolved to write the *Adagio* for the clockmaker at once so that I might drop a few ducats into the hands of my dear little wife; and I began it, but was unlucky enough—because I hate such work—not to be able to finish it. I write at it every day, but have to drop it because it bores me. If the reason for its existence were not such a momentous one, rest assured I should let the thing drop. I hope, however, to force it through in time. Ah, yes! if it were a large clock-work with a sound like an organ I'd be glad to do it; but as it is the thing is made up of tiny pipes only, which sound too shrill and childish for me.

Frankfort-on-the-Main, October 3, 1790, to his wife. "A Piece for an Organ in a Clock" (Köchel's catalogue, No. 594). It was probably ordered by Count Deym for his Wax-works Museum on the occasion of the death of the famous Field Marshal Laudon. The dominant mood of sorrow prevails in the first movement; the *Allegro* is in Händel's style.

CONCERNING THE OPERA

When he was twenty-two years old Mozart wrote to his father, "I am strongly filled with the desire to write an opera." Often does he speak of this ambition. It was, in fact, his true and individual field as the symphony was that of Beethoven. He took counsel with his father by letter touching many details in his earlier operas, wherefore we are advised about their origin, and, what is more to the purpose, about Mozart's fine æsthetic judgment. His four operatic masterpieces are imperishable, and a few words about them are in place, particularly since Mozart has left numerous and interesting comments on "Die Entführung aus dem Serail." This first German opera he composed with the confessed purpose of substituting a work designed for the "national lyric stage" for the conventional and customary Italian opera. Despite its Hispano-Turkish color, the work is so ingenuous, so German in feeling, and above all so full of German humor, that the success was unexampled, and Mozart could write to his father: "The people are daft over my opera." Here, at the very outset, Mozart's humor, the golden one of all the gifts with which Mother Nature had endowed him, was called into play. With this work German comic opera took its beginning. As has been remarked, "although it has been imitated, it has never been surpassed in its musically comic effects." The delightfully Falstaffian figure of *Osmin*, most ingeniously characterized in the music, will create merriment for all time, and the opera acquires a new, personal and peculiarly amiable charm from the fact that we are privileged to see in the love-joy of *Belmont* and *Constanze* an image of that of the young composer and his "Stanzerl."

13

After "Die Entführung" (1782) came "Le Nozze di Figaro" (1786), "Don Giovanni" (1787), and "Die Zauberflöte" (1791). It would be a vain task to attempt to establish any internal relationship between these works. Mozart was not, like Wagner, a strong personality capable of devoting a full sum of vital force to the carrying out of a chosen and approved principle. As is generally the case with geniuses, he was a child; a child led by momentary conditions; moreover, a child of the rococo period. There is, therefore, no cause of wonderment in the fact that Italian texts are again used in "Le Nozze di Figaro" and "Don Giovanni," and that another, but this time a complete German opera, does not appear until we reach "Die Zauberflöte."

Nevertheless, it is possible to note a development towards a climax in the four operas respecting Mozart's conception of the world. It has been denied that there is a single red thread in Mozart's life-work. Nevertheless, our method of study will disclose to us an ever-growing view of human life, and a deeper and deeper glimpse into the emotional and intellectual life of man, his aims and destiny. From the almost commonplace conditions of "Die Entführung," where a rascal sings in the best of humor of first beheading and then hanging a man, we reach a plane in "The Marriage of Figaro," in which despite the refinement and mitigation of Beaumarchais's indictment we feel the revolutionary breeze freshly blowing. In "Don Giovanni" we see the individual set up in opposition to God and the world, in order that he fulfil his destiny, or live out his life, as the popular phrase goes today. Here the tremendous tragedy which lies in the story has received a musical expression quite without parallel, notwithstanding the moderation exercised in the employment of means. In "Die Zauberflöte," finally, we observe the clarification which follows the fermentation. Here we breathe the pure, clear atmosphere of heaven, the atmosphere within which he can live who has freed himself from selfish desire, thus gaining internal peace, and who recognizes his *ego* only in the happiness and welfare of others.

22. I have an unspeakable desire to compose another opera. . . . In Italy one can acquire more honor and credit with an

opera than with a hundred concerts in Germany, and I am the happier because I can compose, which, after all, is my one joy and passion. . . . I am beside myself as soon as I hear anybody talk about an opera, sit in a theatre or hear singing.

Munich, October 11, 1777, to his father, reporting an expectation of making a position for himself in Italy.

23. I beg of you do your best that we may go to Italy. You know my greatest longing—to write operas. . . . Do not forget my wish to write operas! I am envious of every man who composes one; I could almost weep from chagrin whenever I hear or see an aria. But Italian, not German; *seria,* not *buffa.*

Mannheim, February 2, 1778, to his father. Mozart wanted to go with the Weber family (he was in love with Aloysia, his future sister-in-law) to Italy while his father was desirous that he should go to Paris.

24. I am strongly possessed by the desire to write an opera—French rather than German, but Italian rather than either German or French. Wendling's associates are all of the opinion that my compositions would please extraordinarily in Paris. One thing is certain; I would not fear the test. As you know I am able to assimilate and imitate pretty much all styles of composition.

Mannheim, February 7, 1778, to his father. Wendling was a flautist in Mannheim.

25. I assure you that if I get a commission to compose an opera I shall not be frightened. True, the [French] language is of the devil's own making, and I fully appreciate all the difficulties that composers have encountered; but I feel myself as capable of overcoming them as any other composer. *Au contraire,* when I convince myself that all is well with my opera, I feel as if my body were afire—my hands and feet tremble with desire to make the Frenchman value and fear the German. Why is no Frenchman ever commissioned to write a grand opera? Why must it always be a foreigner? In my case the most unendurable thing would be the singers. Well, I'm ready. I shall begin no dickerings, but if I am challenged I shall know how to defend myself. But I should

prefer to get along without a duel; I do not like to fight with dwarfs.

Paris, July 31, 1778, to his father.

26. Do you imagine that I would write an *opéra comique* in the same manner as an *opera seria?* There must be as little learning and seriousness in an *opera buffa* as there must be much of these elements in an *opera seria;* but all the more of playfulness and merriment. I am not responsible for the fact that there is a desire also to hear comic music in an *opera seria;* the difference is sharply drawn here. I find that the buffoon has not been banished from music, and in this respect the French are right.

Vienna, June 16, 1781, to his father. Mozart draws the line of demarcation sharply between tragedy and comedy in opera. ["Shakespeare has taught us to accept an infusion of the comic element in plays of a serious cast; but Shakespeare was an innovator, a Romanticist, and, measured by old standards, his dramas are irregular. The Italians, who followed classic models, for a reason amply explained by the genesis of the art-form, rigorously excluded comedy from serious operas, except as *intermezzi,* until they hit upon a third classification, which they called *opera semiseria,* in which a serious subject was enlivened with comic episodes. Our dramatic tastes being grounded in Shakespeare, we should be inclined to put down 'Don Giovanni' as a musical tragedy; or, haunted by the Italian terminology, as *opera semiseria;* but Mozart calls it *opera buffa,* more in deference to the librettist's work, I fancy, than his own."—*How to Listen to Music,* page 221. H. E. K.]

27. In opera, willy-nilly, poetry must be the obedient daughter of music. Why do Italian operas please everywhere, even in Paris, as I have been a witness, despite the wretchedness of their librettos? Because in them music rules and compels us to forget everything else. All the more must an opera please in which the plot is well carried out, and the words are written simply for the sake of the music and not here and there to please some miserable rhyme, which, God knows, adds nothing to a theatrical representation but more often harms it. Verses are the most indispensable thing in music, but rhymes, for the sake of rhymes, the

most injurious. Those who go to work so pedantically will assuredly come to grief along with the music. It were best if a good composer, who understands the stage, and is himself able to suggest something, and a clever poet could be united in one, like a phœnix. Again, one must not fear the applause of the unknowing.

Vienna, October 13, 1781, to his father. The utterance is notable as showing Mozart's belief touching the relationship between text and music; he places himself in opposition to Gluck whose ideas were at a later day accepted by Wagner. ["It was my intention to confine music to its true dramatic province, of assisting poetical expression, and of augmenting the interest of the fable, without interrupting the action, or chilling it with useless and superfluous ornaments; for the office of music, when joined to poetry, seemed to me to resemble that of coloring in a correct and well disposed design, where the lights and shades only seem to animate the figures without altering the outline."—Gluck in his dedication of "Alceste" to the Grand Duke of Tuscany. "The error in the genre of opera consists herein, that a means of expression (music) has been made the end, while the end of expression (the drama) has been made a means."—Wagner, "Opera and Drama." H. E. K.]

28. *Nota bene,* what has always seemed unnatural in an aria are the asides. In speech one can easily and quickly throw in a few words in an aside; but in an aria, in which the words must be repeated, the effect is bad.

Munich, November 8, 1780, to his father. Mozart had been invited to Munich to compose an opera, "Idomeneo, Re di Creta," for the carnival of 1781. [In contradistinction to the observations touching poetry and music in the preceding paragraph, this remark shows that he nevertheless had a sense of dramatic propriety. He accepted the form as he found it, but protested against the things which stood in the way of its vitalization. H. E. K.]

29. The second duet will be cut out entirely—more for the good than the harm of the opera. You shall see for yourself, if you read over the scene, that it would be weakened and cooled by an aria or duet, which, moreover, would be extremely annoying to the other actors who would have to stand around with nothing to do; besides the magnanimous contest between *Ilia*

and *Idamante* would become too long and therefore lose in value.

Munich, November 13, 1780, to his father. The reference is to the opera "Idomeneo."

30. It will be better to write a recitative under which the instruments can do some good work; for in this scene, which is to be the best in the whole opera, there will be so much noise and confusion on the stage that an aria would cut but a sorry figure. Moreover there will be a thunder-storm which is not likely to cease out of respect for an aria, and the effect of a recitative between two choruses will be incomparably better.

Munich, November 15, to his father. Mozart was at work on "Idomeneo."

31. Don't you think that the speech of the subterranean voice is too long? Think it over, carefully. Imagine the scene on the stage. The voice must be terrifying—it must be impressive, one must believe it real. How can this be so if the speech is too long —the length itself convincing the listener of the fictitiousness of the scene? If the speech of the *Ghost* in "Hamlet" were not so long it would be more effective.

Vienna, November 29, 1780, to his father, who had made the following suggestions respecting the opera "Idomeneo." "*Idamante* and *Ilia* have a short quarrel (near the close of the opera) in a few words of recitative which is interrupted by a subterranean noise, whereupon the oracle speaks also from the depths. The voice and the accompaniment must be moving, terrifying and most extraordinary; it ought to make a masterpiece of harmony."

32. In a word: far-fetched or unusual words are always out of place in an agreeable aria; moreover, I should like to have the aria suggest only restfulness and satisfaction; and if it consisted of only one part I should still be satisfied—in fact, I should prefer to have it so.

Munich, December 5, 1780, to his father. "Idomeneo" is still the subject of discussion.

33. As to the matter of popularity, be unconcerned; there is music in my opera for all sorts of persons—but none for long ears.

Munich, December 16, 1780, to his father, who had expressed a fear that Mozart would not write down to the level of his public. [On December 11, his father had written: "I recommend you not to think in your work only of the musical public, but also of the unmusical. You know that there are a hundred ignorant people for every ten true connoisseurs; so do not forget what is called popular and tickle the long ears." H. E. K.]

34. I have had a good deal of trouble with him about the quartet. The oftener I fancy it performed on the stage the more effective it seems to me; and it has pleased all who have heard it on the pianoforte. Raaff alone thinks it will make no effect. He said to me in private: *"Non c'è da spianar la voce—*it is too curt." As if we should not speak more than we sing in a quartet! He has no understanding of such things. I said to him simply: "My dear friend, if I knew a single note which might be changed in this quartet I would change it at once; but I have not been so completely satisfied with anything in the opera as I am with this quartet; when you have heard it sung together you will talk differently. I have done my best to fit you with the two arias, will do it again with the third, and hope to succeed; but you must let the composer have his own way in trios and quartets." Whereupon he was satisfied. Recently he was vexed because of one of the words in his best aria—*rinvigorir* and *ringiovanir,* particularly *vienmi a rinvigorir—*five i's. It is true it is very unpleasant at the conclusion of an aria.

Munich, December 27, 1780, to his father. Raaff was the principal singer in the opera "Idomeneo," which Mozart had been commissioned to write by the Elector for Munich. The observation shows how capable Mozart was of appreciating foreign criticism.

35. My head and hands are so full of the third act that it would not be strange if I were myself transformed into a third act. It has cost me more care than an entire opera, for there is scarcely a scene in it which is not interesting. The accompani-

ment for the subterranean voice consists of five voices only—three trombones and two French-horns, which are placed at the point from which the voice proceeds. At this moment the whole orchestra is silent.

Munich, January 3, 1781, to his father, whom in the same letter he invites to Munich to hear the opera.

36. After the chorus of mourning the *King,* the populace, everybody, leave the stage, and the next scene begins with the directions: *Idomeneo in ginocchione nel tempio (Idomeneus,* kneeling in the temple). That will never do; he must come with all his following. That necessitates a march, and I have composed a very simple one for two violins, viola, bass and two oboes, which is to be played *a mezza voce,* during which the *King* enters and the *priests* make the preparations for the sacrifice. Then the *King* sinks on his knees and begins his prayer. In *Electra's* recitative, after the subterranean voice, the word *Partono* (they go) should be written in; I forgot to look at the copy made for the printer and do not know whether or how·the direction has been written in. It seems silly to me that everybody should hurry away only in order to leave *Mademoiselle Electra* alone.

Munich, January 3, 1781, to his father.

37. I am glad to compose the book. The time is short, it is true, for it must be performed about the middle of September; but the circumstances connected with the performances, and a number of other purposes, are of such a character that they enliven my spirits in such a degree that I hurry to my writing desk and remain seated there with great joy.

Vienna, August 1, 1781, to his father. The opera referred to is "Die Entführung aus dem Serail." The "circumstances" were the court festivals which were to celebrate the coming of the Russian Grand Duke, from which Mozart, as was his wont, expected all manner of future benefits.

38. As regards the work of Stephanie you are right, of course, but nevertheless the poetry is well fitted to the character of the

stupid, coarse and malicious *Osmin*. I know full well that the style of the verse is none of the best, but it has so adjusted itself to the musical thoughts (which were promenading in my brain in advance) that the lines had to please me, and I will wager there will be no disappointment at the performance. So far as the songs are concerned they are not to be despised. *Belmont's* aria "O, wie ängstlich" could scarcely have been written better for music.

Vienna, October 13, 1781, to his father. Stephanie was the author of the libretto of "Die Entführung aus dem Serail."

39. An aria has been written for *Osmin* in the first act. . . . You have seen only the beginning and end of it, which must be effective; the rage of *Osmin* is made ridiculous by the use of Turkish music. In developing the aria I have given him [Fischer, a bass] a chance to show his beautiful low tones. The "By the beard of the Prophet" remains in the same tempo but has quicker notes, and as his anger grows continually, when one thinks that the aria is come to an end, the *Allegro assai* must make the best kind of an effect when it enters in a different measure and key. Here is the reason: a man who is in such a violent rage oversteps all order, all moderation; he forgets himself, and the music must do the same.

Inasmuch as the passions, whether violent or not, must never be carried in their expression to the verge of disgust, and music, even in the most awful situations, must not offend the ear but always please, consequently always remain music, I have not chosen a key foreign to F [*i.e.* the key of the aria], but a related one, —not the nearest, D minor, but the more distant, A minor. You know how I have given expression to *Belmont's* aria, "O, wie ängstlich, O wie feurig,"—there is a suggestion of the beating heart,—the violins in octaves. This is the favorite aria of all who have heard it,—of myself, as well,—and is written right into the voice of Adamberger. One can see the reeling and trembling, one can see the heaving breast which is illustrated by a *crescendo;* one hears the lispings and sighs expressed by the muted violins with flute in unison. The Janizary chorus is, as such, all that could be asked, short and jolly, written to suit the Viennese.

Vienna, September 26, 1781, to his father. Concerning the composition of "Die Entführung," Mozart delivered himself at greater length and more explicitly than about any other opera. From the above excerpt one can learn his notions touching musical characterization and delineation. ["Turkish" music, or "Janizary" music, is that in which the percussion effects of Oriental music are imitated—music utilizing the large drum, cymbals, etc. H. E. K.]

40. The close will make a deal of noise; and that is all that is necessary for the end of an act;—the noisier the better, the shorter the better, so that the people shall not get too cool to applaud.

Vienna, September 26, 1781, to his father. The Trio at the end of the first act is the finale referred to.

41. My opera is to be performed again next Friday, but I have protested against it as I do not want it to be ridden to death at once. The public, I may say, are daft about this opera. It does a fellow good to receive such applause.

Vienna, July 27, 1782, to his father.

42. My opera was performed again yesterday, this time at the request of Gluck. Gluck paid me many compliments on it. I am to dine with him to-morrow.

Vienna, August 7, 1782, to his father. [How Mozart and Gluck differed in principle on the relation between text and music the reader has already had an opportunity to learn. H. E. K.]

43. The most necessary thing is that the whole be really comical; then, if possible, there should be two equally good female parts, one *seria,* the other *mezzo carattere;* but one must be as good as the other. The third woman may be all *buffa,* also all the men if necessary.

Vienna, May 7, 1783, to his father, in Salzburg, where the Abbé Varesco was to write an opera libretto.

44. It would be a pity if I should have composed this music for nothing, that is to say if no regard is to be shown for things

that are absolutely essential. Neither you, nor Abbé Varesco, nor I, reflected that it will be a bad thing, that the opera will be a failure, in fact, if neither of the principal women appears on the scene until the last minute, but both are kept promenading on the bastion of the fortress. I credit the audience with patience enough for one act, but it would never endure the second. It must not be.

Vienna, December 6, 1783, to his father. The opera in question, entitled "L'Oca del Cairo," was never finished.

45. Abbé Varesco has written over the cavatina for *Lavina: a cui servirà la musica della cavatina antecedente,*—that is the cavatina of *Celidora*. But that will never do. In *Celidora's* cavatina the words are comfortless and hopeless, while in *Lavina's* cavatina they are full of comfort and hope. Moreover it is hackneyed and no longer customary habit to let one singer echo the song of another. At best it might only be done by a soubrette and her sweetheart at *ultime parti*.

Vienna, December 24, 1783, to his father. The Italian phrase is a direction that the music of a preceding cavatina might be used for a second cavatina.

46. It is much more natural, since they have all come to an agreement in the quartetto to carry out their plan of attack that the men leave the stage to gather their helpers together, and the women quietly retire to their retreat. All that can be allowed them is a few lines of recitative.

Vienna, December 24, 1783, to his father. The situation referred to was in Varesco's opera which never reached completion.

47. At six o'clock I drove with Count Canal to the so-called "Breitfeldischen Ball" where the pick of the beauties of Prague are in the habit of congregating. That would have been something for you, my friend! I fancy seeing you,—not walking, but limping,—after all the pretty girls and women! I did not dance, neither did I spoon;—the first because I was too tired, the second because of my congenital bashfulness. But I saw with great pleas-

ure how all these people hopped about delightedly to the music of my "Figaro" turned into contradances and Allemands. Here nothing is talked about except "Figaro," nothing played, piped, sung or whistled except "Figaro;" no opera is attended except "Figaro," always "Figaro." Certainly a great honor for me.

Prague, January 15, 1787, to a friend, whose name is unknown.

48. "Don Giovanni" was not written for the Viennese; rather for the people of Prague, but most of all for me and my friends.

Reported by Nissen, who also relates that Mozart often said "The Bohemians are the ones who understand me." When "Le Nozze di Figaro" received an enthusiastic reception in Prague, Mozart said: "Because the Bohemians understand me so well I must write an opera for them." The opera was "Don Giovanni."

49. I am just home from the opera; it was as crowded as ever. The duet, "Mann und Weib," and the bells in the first act, were repeated as usual,—also the trio of the boys in the second act. But what delights me most is the silent applause! It is easy to see how this opera is ever rising.

Vienna, October 7, 1791, to his wife. The opera was "Die Zauberflöte."

MUSICAL PEDAGOGICS

50. Herr Stein is completely daft on the subject of his daughter. She is eight years old and learns everything by heart. Something may come of her for she has talent, but not if she goes on as she is doing now; she will never acquire velocity because she purposely makes her hand heavy. She will never learn the most necessary, most difficult and principal thing in music, that is time, because from childhood she has designedly cultivated the habit of ignoring the beat.

Augsburg, October 23, 1777, to his father. Nanette Stein afterward married Andreas Streicher, who was Schiller's companion in his flight to Franconia. As Frau Streicher she became Beethoven's faithful friend and frequently took it upon herself to straighten out his domestic affairs.

51. If she docs not get some thoughts and ideas (for now she has absolutely none), it will all be in vain, for God knows, I can not give her any. It is not her father's intention to make a great composer out of her. "She shall," he says, "not write any operas, or arias, or symphonies, but only great sonatas for her instrument and mine!" I gave her her fourth lesson to-day, and so far as the rules of composition and her exercises are concerned I am pretty well satisfied with her. She wrote a very good bass to the first minuet which I set her, and has already begun to write in three parts. It goes, but she gets bored too quickly. I can not help her; progress is impossible, she is too young even if she had talent. Unfortunately she has none; she must be taught artificially; she has no ideas, there are no results, I have tried in every sort of way. Among other things it occurred to me to write down a very

25

simple minuet and to see if she could write a variation on it. In vain. Well, thought I, it is because she does not know how to begin. I then began a variation of the first measure and told her to continue it in the same manner; that went fairly well. When she had made an end I asked her to begin something of her own, —only the first voice, a melody. She thought a full quarter of an hour, and nothing came. Thereupon I wrote four measures of a minuet and said to her: "Now look what an ass I am; I have begun a minuet and can't finish even the first part; be good enough to finish it for me." She thought it impossible. At length she produced a little something to my joy. Then I made her finish the minuet, *i.e.* only the first voice. For her home work I have given her nothing to do except to alter my four measures and make something out of them, to invent another beginning, to keep to the harmony if she must, but to write a new melody. We shall see what comes of it to-morrow.

Paris, May 14, 1778, to his father. The pupil was the daughter of the Duke de Guines, an excellent flautist. "She plays the harp magnificently," writes Mozart in the same letter; "has a great deal of talent and genius, and an incomparable memory. She knows 200 pieces and plays them all by heart." When it came to paying Mozart for the lessons the Duke was anything but a nobleman.

52. The *Andante* is going to give us the most trouble, for it is full of expression and must be played with taste and accurately as written in the matter of *forte* and *piano*. She is very clever and learns quickly. The right hand is very good but the left utterly ruined. I can say that I often pity her when I see that she is obliged to labor till she gasps, not because she is unapt, but because she can't help it,—she is used to playing so, nobody ever taught her differently. I said to her mother and her that if I were her regular teacher, I would lock up all her music, cover the keyboard with a handkerchief, and make her practise both hands at first slowly on nothing but passages, trills, mordents, etc., until the difficulty with the left hand was remedied; after that I am sure I could make a real clavier player out of her. It is a pity; she has so much genius, reads respectably, has a great deal of natural fluency and plays with a great deal of feeling.

Mannheim, November 16, 1777, to his father. The pupil was Rose Cannabich, to whom the sonata referred to is dedicated. Her father, whom Mozart admired greatly as an able conductor, was Chapelmaster of the excellently trained orchestra at Mannheim. He lived from 1731 to 1798. [The *Andante* from which trouble was expected was that which Mozart wrote with the purpose that it should reflect the character of Rose Cannabich, a lovely and amiable girl, according to all accounts. H. E. K.]

53. This E is very forced. One can see that it was written only to go from one consonance to another in parallel motion,—just as bad poets write nonsense for the sake of a rhyme.

From the exercise book of the cousin of Abbé Stadler who took lessons in thorough-bass from Mozart in 1784. It is preserved in the Court Library in Vienna.

54. My good lad, you ask my advice and I will give it you candidly; had you studied composition when you were at Naples, and when your mind was not devoted to other pursuits, you would, perhaps, have done wisely; but now that your profession of the stage must, and ought to, occupy all your attention, it would be an unwise measure to enter into a dry study. You may take my word for it, Nature has made you a melodist, and you would only disturb and perplex yourself. Reflect, "a little knowledge is a dangerous thing;"—should there be errors in what you write, you will find hundreds of musicians in all parts of the world capable of correcting them, therefore do not disturb your natural gift.

To Michael Kelly, the Irish tenor, to whom Mozart assigned the parts of *Basilio* and *Don Curzio* at the first performance of "Le Nozze di Figaro" in 1786. Kelly had asked Mozart whether or not he should study counterpoint. [See No. 8. Three years later Kelly returned to England, began his career as composer of musical pieces for the stage. He was fairly prolific, but failed to impress the public with the originality of his creative talent. He went into the wine business, which fact led Sheridan to make the witty suggestion that he inscribe over his shop: "Michael Kelly, Composer of Wines and Importer of Music." He was born in 1764 and died in 1826. H. E. K.]

55. This is generally the case with all who did not taste the rod or feel the teacher's tongue when boys, and later think that they can compel things to their wishes by mere talent and inclination. Many succeed fairly well, but with other people's ideas, having none of their own; others who have ideas of their own, do not know what to do with them. That is your case.

In a letter written in 1789 to a noble friend criticising a symphony.

56. Do not wonder at me; it was not a caprice. I noticed that most of the musicians were old men. There would have been no end of dragging if I had not first driven them into the fire and made them angry. Out of pure rage they did their best.

Reported by Rochlitz. Mozart was rehearsing the *Allegro* of one of his symphonies in Leipsic. He worked up such a fit of anger that he stamped his foot and broke one of his shoe-laces. His anger fled and he broke into a merry laugh.

57. Right! That's the way to shriek.

At a rehearsal of "Don Giovanni" the representative of *Zerlina* did not act realistically enough to suit Mozart. Thereupon he went unnoticed on the stage and at the repetition of the scene grabbed the singer so rudely and unexpectedly that she involuntarily uttered the shriek which the scene called for. [The singer was Teresa Bondini, the place Prague, and the time before the first performance of the opera which took place on October 29, 1787. H. E. K.]

TOUCHING MUSICAL
PERFORMANCES

58. Herr Stein sees and hears that I am more of a player than Beecké,—that without making grimaces of any kind I play so expressively that, according to his own confession, no one shows off his pianoforte as well as I. That I always remain strictly in time surprises every one; they can not understand that the left hand should not in the least be concerned in a *tempo rubato*. When they play the left hand always follows.

Augsburg, October 23, 1777, to his father. [We have here a suggestion of the *tempo rubato* as played by Chopin according to the testimony of Mikuli, who said that no matter how free Chopin was either in melody or arabesque with his right hand, the left always adhered strictly to the time. Mozart learned the principle from his father who in his method for the violin condemned the accompanists who spoiled the *tempo rubato* of an artist by waiting to follow him. H. E. K.]

59. Whoever can see and hear her (the daughter of Stein) play without laughing must be a stone (*Stein*) like her father. She sits opposite the treble instead of in the middle of the instrument, so that there may be greater opportunities for swaying about and making grimaces. Then she rolls up her eyes and smirks. If a passage occurs twice it is played slower the second time; if three times, still slower. When a passage comes, up goes the arm, and if there is to be an emphasis it must come from the arm, heavily and clumsily, not from the fingers. But the best of all is that when there comes a passage (which ought to flow like oil) in which there necessarily occurs a change of fingers, there is

no need of taking care; when the time comes you stop, lift the hand and nonchalantly begin again. This helps one the better to catch a false note, and the effect is frequently curious.

Augsburg, October 23, 1777. The letter is to his father and the young woman whose playing is criticised is the little miss of eight years, Nanette Stein.

60. When I told Herr Stein that I would like to play on his organ and that I was passionately fond of the instrument, he marvelled greatly and said: "What, a man like you, so great a clavier player, want to play on an instrument which has no *douceur*, no expression, neither *piano* nor *forte*, but goes on always the same?" "But all that signifies nothing; to me the organ is nevertheless the king of instruments."

Augsburg, October 17, 1777, to his father.

61. I had the pleasure to hear Herr Franzl (whose wife is a sister of Madame Cannabich) play a concerto on the violin. He pleases me greatly. You know that I am no great lover of difficulties. He plays difficult things, but one does not recognize that they are difficult, but imagines that one could do the same thing at once; that is true art. He also has a beautiful, round tone,—not a note is missing, one hears everything; everything is well marked. He has a fine *staccato* bow, up as well as down; and I have never heard so good a double shake as his. In a word, though he is no wizard he is a solid violinist.

Mannheim, November 22, 1777, to his father.

62. Wherein consists the art of playing *prima vista?* In this: To play in the proper tempo; give expression to every note, appoggiatura, etc., tastefully and as they are written, so as to create the impression that the player had composed the piece.

Mannheim, January 17, 1778, to his father. Mozart had just been sharply criticising the playing of Abbé Vogler. (See No. 66.)

63. I am at Herr von Aurnhammer's after dinner nearly every day. The young woman is a fright, but she plays ravishingly,

though she lacks the true singing style in the *cantabile;* she is too jerky.

Vienna, June 27, 1781, to his father. Beethoven found the same fault with Mozart's playing that Mozart here condemns.

64. Herr Richter plays much and well so far as execution is concerned, but—as you will hear—crudely, laboriously and without taste or feeling; he is one of the best fellows in the world, and without a particle of vanity. Whenever I played for him he looked immovably at my fingers, and one day he said, "My God! how I am obliged to torment myself and sweat, and yet without obtaining applause; and for you, my friend, it is mere play!" "Yes," said I, "I had to labor once in order not to show labor now."

Vienna, April 28, 1784, to his father in Salzburg, whither the pianist Richter, whom he recommends to his father, is going on a concert trip.

65. Meissner, as you know, has the bad habit of purposely making his voice tremble, marking thus entire quarter and eighth notes; I never could endure it in him. It is indeed despicable and contrary to all naturalness in song. True, the human voice trembles of itself, but only in a degree that remains beautiful; it is in the nature of the voice. We imitate it not only on wind instruments but also on the viols and even on the clavier. But as soon as you overstep the limit it is no longer beautiful because it is contrary to nature.

Paris, June 12, 1778, to his father. [The statement that the *tremolo* effect could be imitated on the clavier seems to require an explanation. Mozart obviously had in view, not the pianoforte which was just coming into use in his day, but the clavichord. This instrument was sounded by striking the strings with bits of brass placed in the farther end of the keys, which were simple and direct levers. The tangents, as they were called, had to be held against the strings as long as it was desired that the tone should sound, and by gently repeating the pressure on the key a tremulousness was imparted to the tone which made the clavichord a more expressive instrument than the harpsichord or the early pianoforte. The effect was called *Bebung* in German, and *Balancement* in French. H. E. K.]

66. Before dinner Herr Vogler dashed through my sonata *prima vista.* He played the first movement *prestissimo,* the andante *allegro* and the rondo *prestissimo* with a vengeance. As a rule, he played a different bass than the one I had written, and occasionally he changed the harmony as well as the melody. That was inevitable, for at such speed the eyes can not follow, nor the hands grasp, the music. Such playing at sight and . . . are all one to me. The hearers (I mean those worthy of the name) can say nothing more than that they have seen music and clavier playing. You can imagine that it was all the more unendurable because I did not dare to say to him: *"Much too quick!"* Moreover it is much easier to play rapidly than slowly; you can drop a few notes in passages without any one noticing it. But is it beautiful? At such speed you can use the hands indiscriminately; but is that beautiful?

   Mannheim, January 17, 1778, to his father.

67. They hurry the tempo, trill or pile on the adornments because they can neither study nor sustain a tone.

   Recorded by Rochlitz as a criticism by Mozart of Italian singers in 1789.

68. It is thus, they think, that they can infuse warmth and ardor into their singing. Ah, if there is no fire in the composition you will surely never get it in by hurrying it.

   According to Rochlitz Mozart used these words while complaining of the manner in which his compositions were ruined by exaggerated speed in the tempi.

EXPRESSIONS CRITICAL

69. We wish that it were in our power to introduce the German taste in minuets in Italy; minuets here last almost as long as whole symphonies.

Bologna, September 22, 1770, to his mother and sister. Mozart as a lad was making a tour through Italy with his father. [There might be a valuable hint here touching the proper tempo for the minuets in Mozart's symphonies. Of late years the conductors, of the Wagnerian school more particularly, have acted on the belief that the symphonic minuets of Mozart and Haydn must be played with the stately slowness of the old dance. Mozart himself was plainly of another opinion. H. E. K.]

70. Beecké told me (and it is true) that music is now played in the cabinet of the Emperor [Joseph II] bad enough to set the dogs a-running. I remarked that unless I quickly escape such music I get a headache. "It doesn't hurt me in the least; bad music leaves my nerves unaffected, but I sometimes get a headache from good music." Then I thought to myself: Yes, such a shallow-pate as you feels a pain as soon as he hears something which he can not understand.

Mannheim, November 13, 1777, to his father. Beecké was a conceited pianist.

71. Nothing gives me so much pleasure in the anticipation as the *Concert spirituel* in Paris, for I fancy I shall be called on to compose something. The orchestra is said to be large and good, and my principal favorites can be well performed there, that is to say choruses, and I am right glad that the Frenchmen are fond

of them. . . . Heretofore Paris has been used to the choruses of Gluck. Depend on me; I shall labor with all my powers to do honor to the name of Mozart.

> Mannheim, February 28, 1778, to his father. On March 7 he writes: "I have centered all my hopes on Paris, for the German princes are all niggards."

72. I do not know whether or not my symphony pleases, and, to tell you the truth, I don't much care. Whom should it please? I warrant it will please the few sensible Frenchmen who are here, and there will be no great misfortune if it fails to please the stupids. Still I have some hope that the asses too will find something in it to their liking.

> Paris, June 12, 1778, to his father. The symphony is that known as the "Parisian" (Köchel, No. 297). It is characterized by brevity and wealth of melody.

73. The most of the symphonies are not to the local taste. If I find time I shall revise a few violin concertos,—shorten them,— for our taste in Germany is for long things; as a matter of fact, short and good is better.

> Paris, September 11, 1778, to his father, in Salzburg. In the same letter he says: "I assure you the journey was not unprofitable to me— that is to say in the matter of composition."

74. If only this damned French language were not so ill adapted to music! It is abominable; German is divine in comparison. And then the singers!—men and women—they are unmentionable. They do not sing; they shriek, they howl with all their might, through throat, nose and gullet.

> Paris, July 9, 1778, to his father. Mozart was thinking of writing a French opera.

75. Ah, if we too had clarinets! You can't conceive what a wonderful effect a symphony with flutes, oboes and clarinets makes. At the first audience with the Archbishop I shall have much to tell him, and, probably, a few suggestions to make. Alas! our

music might be much better and more beautiful if only the Archbishop were willing.

Mannheim, December 3, 1778, to his father. Mozart was on his return to Salzburg where he had received an appointment in the Archiepiscopal chapel. It seems that wood-wind instruments were still absent from the symphony orchestra in Salzburg.

76. Others know as well as you and I that tastes are continually changing, and that the changes extend even into church music; this should not be, but it accounts for the fact that true church music is now found only in the attic and almost eaten up by the worms.

Vienna, April 12, 1783, to his father, who was active as Court Chapelmaster in Salzburg, and who had been asked by his son in the same letter, when it grew a little warmer, "to look in the attic and send some of your [his] church music."

77. The themes pleased me most in the symphony; yet it will be the least effective, for there is too much in it, and a fragmentary performance of it sounds like an ant hill looks,—that is as if the devil had been turned loose in it.

In a letter written in 1789 to a nobleman who was a composer and had submitted a symphony to Mozart for criticism.

78. So far as melody is concerned, yes; for dramatic effect, no. Moreover the scores which you may see here, outside those of Grétry, are by Gluck, Piccini and Salieri, and there is nothing French about them except the words.

A remark made to Joseph Frank, whom Mozart frequently found occupied with French scores, and who had asked whether the study of Italian scores were not preferable.

79. The ode is elevated, beautiful, everything you wish, but too exaggerated and bombastic for my ears. But what would you? The golden mean, the truth, is no longer recognized or valued. To win applause one must write stuff so simple that a coachman might sing it after you, or so incomprehensible that it pleases

simply because no sensible man can comprehend it. But it is not this that I wanted to discuss with you, but another matter. I have a strong desire to write a book, a little work on musical criticism with illustrative examples. N. B., not under my name.

Vienna, December 28, 1782, to his father. "I was working on a very difficult task—a Bardic song by Denis on Gibraltar. It is a secret, for a Hungarian lady wants thus to honor Denis." When Gibraltar was gallantly defended against the Spaniards, Mozart's father wrote to him calling his attention to the victory. Mozart replied: "Yes, I have heard of England's triumph, and, indeed, with great joy (for you know well that I am an arch-Englishman)." The little book of criticism never appeared.

80. The orchestra in Berlin contains the greatest aggregation of *virtuosi* in the world; I never heard such quartet playing as here; but when all the gentlemen are together they might do better.

To King Frederick William II, in 1789, when asked for an opinion on the orchestra in Berlin. The king asked Mozart to transfer his services to the Court at Berlin; Mozart replied: "Shall I forsake my good Emperor?"

OPINIONS CONCERNING OTHERS

81. Holzbauer's music is very beautiful; the poetry is not worthy of it. What amazes me most is that so old a man as Holzbauer should have so much spirit,—it is incredible, the amount of fire in his music.

Mannheim, November 14, 1777, to his father. Ignaz Holzbauer was born in Vienna, in 1711, and died as Chapelmaster in Mannheim, on April 7, 1793. During the last years of his life he was totally deaf. The music referred to was the setting of the first great German *Singspiel*, "Günther von Schwarzburg."

82. There is much that is pretty in many of Martini's things, but in ten years nobody will notice them.

Reported by Nissen. Martini lived in Bologna from 1706 to 1784; there Mozart learned to know and admire him. In 1776 he wrote a letter to him in which he said that of all people in the world he "loved, honored and valued" him most.

83. For those who seek only light entertainment in music nobody better can be recommended than Paisiello.

Reported by Nissen. Paisiello was born in Taranto in 1741, composed over a hundred operas which, like his church music, won much applause. He died in Naples in 1816. Mozart considered his music "transparent."

84. Jomelli has his genre in which he shines, and we must abandon the thought of supplanting him in that field in the judgment of the knowing. But he ought not to have abandoned his field to compose church music in the old style, for instance.

Reported by Nissen. Jomelli was born in 1714 near Naples, where he died in 1774. He was greatly admired as a composer of operas and church music. He was Court Chapelmaster in Stuttgart from 1753 to 1769.

85. Wait till you know how many of his works we have in Vienna! When I get back home I shall diligently study his church music, and I hope to learn a great deal from it.

A remark made in Leipsic when somebody spoke slightingly of the music of Gassmann, an Imperial Court Chapelmaster in Vienna, and much respected by Maria Theresa and Joseph.

86. The fact that Gatti, the ass, begged the Archbishop for permission to compose a serenade shows his worthiness to wear the title, which I make no doubt he deserves also for his musical learning.

Vienna, October 12, 1782, to his father. Gatti was Cathedral Chapelmaster in Salzburg.

87. What we should like to have, dear father, is some of your best church pieces; for we love to entertain ourselves with all manner of masters, ancient and modern. Therefore I beg of you send us something of yours as soon as possible.

Vienna, March 29, 1783, to his father, Leopold Mozart in Salzburg, himself a capable composer.

88. In a sense Vogler is nothing but a wizard. As soon as he attempts to play something majestic he becomes dry, and you are glad that he, too, feels bored and makes a quick ending. But what follows?—unintelligible slip-slop. I listened to him from a distance. Afterward he began a fugue with six notes on the same tone, and *Presto!* Then I went up to him. As a matter of fact I would rather watch him than hear him.

Mannheim, December 18, 1777, to his father. Abbé Vogler was trying the new organ in the Lutheran church at Mannheim. Vogler lived from 1749 to 1814, and was the teacher of Carl Maria von Weber (who esteemed him highly) and Meyerbeer. Mozart's criticism seems unduly severe.

89. I was at mass, a brand new composition by Vogler. I had already been at the rehearsal day before yesterday afternoon, but went away after the *Kyrie*. In all my life I have heard nothing like this. Frequently everything is out of tune. He goes from key to key as if he wanted to drag one along by the hair of the head, not in an interesting manner which might be worth while, but bluntly and rudely. As to the manner in which he develops his ideas I shall say nothing; but this I will say, that it is impossible for a mass by Vogler to please any composer worthy of the name. Briefly, I hear a theme which is not bad; does it long remain not bad, think you? will it not soon become beautiful? Heaven forefend! It grows worse and worse in a two-fold or three-fold manner; for instance, scarcely is it begun before something else enters and spoils it; or he makes so unnatural a close that it can not remain good; or it is misplaced; or, finally, it is ruined by the orchestration. That's Vogler's music.

Mannheim, November 20, 1777, to his father.

90. Clementi plays well so far as execution with the right hand is concerned; his forte is passages in thirds. Aside from this he hasn't a pennyworth of feeling or taste; in a word he is a mere mechanician.

Vienna, January 12, 1782, to his father. Four days later Mozart expressed the same opinion of Muzio Clementi, who is still in good repute, after having met him in competition before the emperor. "Clementi preluded and played a sonata; then the Emperor said to me, '*Allons*, go ahead.' I preluded and played some variations."

91. Now I must say a few words to my sister about the Clementi sonatas. Every one who plays or hears them will feel for himself that as compositions they do not signify. There are in them no remarkable or striking passages, with the exception of those in sixths and octaves, and I beg my sister not to devote too much time to these lest she spoil her quiet and steady hand and make it lose its natural lightness, suppleness and fluent rapidity. What, after all, is the use? She is expected to play the sixths and octaves with the greatest velocity (which no man will accomplish, not even Clementi), and if she tries she will produce a frightful

zig-zag, and nothing more. Clementi is a *Ciarlatano* like all Italians. He writes upon a sonata *Presto*, or even *Prestissimo* and *alla breve*, and plays it *Allegro* in 4-4 time. I know it because I have heard him! What he does well is his passages in thirds; but he perspired over these day and night in London. Aside from this he has nothing,—absolutely nothing; not excellence in reading, nor taste, nor sentiment.

Vienna, June 7, 1783, to his father and sister.

92. Händel knows better than any of us what will make an effect; when he chooses he strikes like a thunderbolt; even if he is often prosy, after the manner of his time, there is always something in his music.

Mozart valued Händel most highly. He knew his masterpieces by heart—not only the choruses but also many arias. [Reported by Rochlitz. H. E. K.]

93. *Apropos,* I intended, while asking you to send back the rondo, to send me also the six fugues by Händel and the toccatas and fugues by Eberlin. I go every Sunday to Baron von Swieten's, and there nothing is played except Händel and Bach. I am making a collection of the fugues,—those of Sebastian as well as of Emanuel and Friedemann Bach; also of Händel's, and here the six are lacking. Besides I want to let the baron hear those of Eberlin. In all likelihood you know that the English Bach is dead; a pity for the world of music.

Vienna, April 10, 1782, to his father. Johann Ernst Eberlin (Eberle), born in 1702, died in 1762 as Archiepiscopal Chapelmaster in Salzburg. Many of his unpublished works are preserved in Berlin. The "English" Bach was Johann Christian, son of the great Johann Sebastian. As a child Mozart made his acquaintance in London.

94. I shall be glad if papa has not yet had the works of Eberlin copied, for I have gotten them meanwhile, and discovered,—for I could not remember,—that they are too trivial and surely do not deserve a place among those of Bach and Händel. All respect to his four-part writing, but his clavier fugues are nothing but long-drawn-out *versetti*.

Vienna, April 29, 1782, to his sister Nannerl.

95. Johann Christian Bach has been here [Paris] for a fortnight. He is to write a French opera, and is come only to hear the singers, whereupon he will go to London, write the opera, and come back to put it on the stage. You can easily imagine his delight and mine when we met again. Perhaps his delight was not altogether sincere, but one must admit that he is an honorable man and does justice to all. I love him, as you know, with all my heart, and respect him; as for him, one thing is certain, that to my face and to others, he really praised me, not extravagantly, like some, but seriously and in earnest.

St. Germain, August 27, 1778, to his father. Johann Christian Bach was the second son of Johann Sebastian, and born in 1735. He lived in London, where little Wolfgang learned to know him in 1764. Bach took the precocious boy on his knee and the two played on the harpsichord. [Bach was Music Master to the Queen. "He liked to play with the boy," says Jahn; "took him upon his knee and went through a sonata with him, each in turn playing a measure with such precision that no one would have suspected two performers. He began a fugue, which Wolfgang took up and completed when Bach broke off." H. E. K.]

96. Bach is the father, we are the youngsters. Those of us who can do a decent thing learned how from him; and whoever will not admit it is a . . .

A remark made at a gathering in Leipsic. The Bach referred to is Phillip Emanuel Bach, who died in 1788.

97. Here, at last, is something from which one can learn!

Mozart's ejaculation when he heard Bach's motet for double chorus, *"Singet dem Herrn ein neues Lied,"* at Leipsic in 1789. Rochlitz relates: "Scarcely had the choir sung a couple of measures when Mozart started. After a few more measures he cried out: 'What is that?' and now his whole soul seemed to be in his ears."

98. Melt us two together, and we will fall far short of making a Haydn.

Said to the pianist Leopold Kozeluch who had triumphantly pointed out a few slips due to carelessness in Haydn's compositions.

99. It was a duty that I owed to Haydn to dedicate my quartets to him; for it was from him that I learned how to write quartets.

Reported by Nissen. Joseph Haydn once said, when the worth of "Don Giovanni" was under discussion: "This I do know, that Mozart is the greatest composer in the world to-day."

100. Nobody can do everything,—jest and terrify, cause laughter or move profoundly,—like Joseph Haydn.

Reported by Nissen [the biographer who married Mozart's widow. H. E. K.].

101. Keep your eyes on him; he'll make the world talk of himself some day!

A remark made by Mozart in reference to Beethoven in the spring of 1787. It was the only meeting between the two composers. [The prophetic observation was called out by Beethoven's improvisation on a theme from "Le Nozze di Figaro." H. E. K.]

102. Attwood is a young man for whom I have a sincere affection and esteem; he conducts himself with great propriety, and I feel much pleasure in telling you that he partakes more of my style than any scholar I ever had, and I predict that he will prove a sound musician.

Remarked in 1786 to Michael Kelly, who was a friend of Attwood and a pupil of Mozart at the time. [Thomas Attwood was an English musician, born in 1765. He was chorister of the Chapel Royal at the age of nine, and at sixteen attracted the attention of the Prince of Wales, afterward George IV, who sent him to Italy to study. He studied two years in Naples and one year in Vienna with Mozart. Returned to London, he first composed for the theatre and afterward largely for the church. He and Mendelssohn were devoted friends. H. E. K.]

103. If the oboist Fischer did not play better when we heard him in Holland (1766) than he plays now, he certainly does not

deserve the reputation which he has. Yet, between ourselves, I was too young at the time to pronounce a judgment; I remember that he pleased me exceedingly, and the whole world. It is explained easily enough if one but realizes that tastes have changed mightily since then. You would think that he plays according to the old school; but no! he plays like a wretched pupil. . . . And then his concertos, his compositions! Every ritornello lasts a quarter of an hour; then the hero appears, lifts one leaden foot after the other and plumps them down alternately. His tone is all nasal, and his *tenuto* sounds like an organ tremulant.

Vienna, April 4, 1787, to his father. Johann Christian Fischer—1733-1800—was a famous oboist and composer for his instrument. [Fischer was probably the original of the many artists of whom the story is told that, having been invited by a nobleman to dinner, he was asked if he had brought his instrument with him, and replied that he had not, for that his instrument never ate. Kelly tells the story in his "Reminiscences" and makes Fischer the hero. H. E. K.]

104. I know nothing new except that Gellert has died in Leipsic and since then has written no more poetry.

Milan, January 26, 1770. Wolfgang was on a concert tour with his father who admired Gellert's writings and had once exchanged letters with him. The lad seems to have felt ironical.

105. Now I am also acquainted with Herr Wieland; but he doesn't know me as well as I know him, for he has not heard anything of mine. I never imagined him to be as he is. He seems to me to be a little affected in speech, has a rather childish voice, a fixed stare, a certain learned rudeness, yet, at times, a stupid condescension. I am not surprised that he behaves as he does here (and as he would not dare do in Weimar or elsewhere), for the people look at him as if he had fallen direct from heaven. All stand in awe, no one talks, everyone is silent, every word is listened to when he speaks. It is a pity that he keeps people in suspense so long, for he has a defect of speech which compels him to speak very slowly and pause after every six words. Otherwise his is, as we all know, an admirable brain. His face is very ugly, pockmarked, and his nose rather long. He is a little taller than papa.

Mannheim, December 27, 1777, to his father. On November 2., Mozart had reported: "In the coming carnival 'Rosamunde' will be performed—new poetry by Herr Wieland, new music by Herr Schweitzer." On January 10, 1778, he writes: " 'Rosamunde' was rehearsed in the theatre to-day; it is—good, but nothing more. If it were bad you could not perform it at all; just as you can't sleep without going to bed!"

106. Now that Herr Wieland has seen me twice he is entirely enchanted. The last time we met, after lauding me as highly as possible, he said, "It is truly a piece of good fortune for me to have met you here," and pressed my hand.

Mannheim, January 10, 1778.

107. Now I give you a piece of news which perhaps you know already; that godless fellow and arch-rascal, Voltaire, is dead— died like a dog, like a beast. That is his reward!

Paris, July 3, 1778, to his father, who, like the son, was a man of sincere piety and abhorred Voltaire's atheism.

108. When God gives a man an office he also gives him sense; that's the case with the Archduke. Before he was a priest he was much wittier and intelligent; spoke less but more sensibly. You ought to see him now! Stupidity looks out of his eyes, he talks and chatters eternally and always in falsetto. His neck is swollen, —in short he has been completely transformed.

Vienna, November 17, 1781, to his father. The person spoken of was Archduke Maximilian, who afterward became Archbishop of Cologne, and was the patron of Beethoven. [The ambiguity of the opening statement is probably due to carelessness in writing, or Mozart's habit of using double negatives. H. E. K.]

WOLFGANG, THE GERMAN

Mozart's Germanism is a matter of pride to the German people. To him "German" was no empty concept, as it was to the majority of his contemporaries. He is therefore honored as a champion of German character and German art, worthy as such to stand beside Richard Wagner. Properly to appreciate his patriotism it is necessary to bear in mind that in Mozart's day Germany was a figment of the imagination, the French language, French manners and Italian music being everywhere dominant. Wagner, on the contrary, was privileged to see the promise of the fulfillment of his strivings in the light of the German victories of 1870-1871. When the genius of Germany soared aloft she carried Wagner with her; Wagner's days of glory in August, 1876, were preconditioned by the great war with France. How insignificant must the patronage of Joseph II, scantily enough bestowed on Mozart in comparison with that showered on Salieri, appear, when we recall the Mæcenas Ludwig II.

109. Frequently I fall into a mood of complete listlessness and indifference; nothing gives me great pleasure. The most stimulating and encouraging thought is that you, dearest father, and my dear sister, are well, that I am an honest German, and that if I am not always permitted to talk I can think what I please; but that is all.

Paris, May 29, 1778, to his father.

110. The Duke de Guines was utterly without a sense of honor and thought that here was a young fellow, and a stupid German to boot,—as all Frenchmen think of the Germans,—he'll be glad

to take it. But the stupid German was not glad and refused to take the money. For two lessons he wanted to pay me the fee of one.

Paris, July 31, 1778, to his father. Mozart had given lessons in composition to the Duke's daughter. See No. 51.

111. An Italian ape, such as he is, who has lived in German countries and eaten German bread for years, ought to speak German, or mangle it, as well or ill as his French mouth will permit.

Said of the violoncellist Duport, the favorite of King William I of Prussia, in 1789, when Mozart was in Berlin and Duport asked him to speak French.

112. I pray God every day to give me grace to remain steadfast here, that I may do honor to myself and the entire German nation, to His greater honor and glory, and that He permit me to make my fortune so that I may help you out of your sorry condition, and bring it to pass that we soon meet again and live together in happiness and joy. But His will be done on earth as in heaven.

Paris, May 1, 1778, to his father who had plunged himself in debt and was giving lessons in order to promote the career of his son. His sister also helped nobly.

113. If this were a place where the people had ears, hearts to feel, and a modicum of musical understanding and taste, I should laugh heartily at all these things; as it is I am among nothing but cattle and brutes (so far as music is concerned). How should it be otherwise since they are the same in all their acts and passions? There is no place like Paris. You must not think that I exaggerate when I talk thus of music. Turn to whom you please,—except to a born Frenchman,—you shall hear the same thing, provided you can find some one to turn to. Now that I am here I must endure out of regard for you. I shall thank God Almighty if I get out of here with a sound taste.

Paris, May 1, 1778.

114. How popular I would be if I were to lift the national German stage to recognition in music! And this would surely happen for I was already full of desire to write when I heard the German *Singspiel.*

Munich, October 2, 1777. [A *Singspiel* is a German opera with spoken dialogue. H. E. K.]

115. If there were but a single patriot on the boards with me, a different face would be put on the matter. Then, mayhap, the budding National Theatre would blossom, and that would be an eternal disgrace to Germany,—if we Germans should once begin to think German, act German, speak German, and—even sing German! ! !

Vienna, March 21, 1785, to the playwright Anton Klein of Mannheim. It was purposed to open the *Singspiel* theatre in October.

116. The German Opera is to be opened in October. For my part I am not promising it much luck. From the doings so far it looks as if an effort were making thoroughly to destroy the German opera which had suspended, perhaps only for a while, rather than to help it up again and preserve it. Only my sister-in-law Lange has been engaged for the German *Singspiel.* Cavalieri, Adamberger, Teyber, all Germans, of whom Germany can be proud, must remain with the Italian opera, must make war against their countrymen!

Vienna, March 21, 1785, to Anton Klein. Madame Lange was Aloysia Weber, with whom Mozart was in love before he married her sister Constanze.

117. The gentlemen of Vienna (including most particularly the Emperor) must not be permitted to believe that I live only for the sake of Vienna. There is no monarch on the face of the earth whom I would rather serve than the Emperor, but I shall not beg service. I believe that I am capable of doing honor to any court. If Germany, my beloved fatherland, of whom you know I am proud, will not accept me, then must I, in the name of God, again make France or England richer by one capable German;— and to the shame of the German nation. You know full well that

in nearly all the arts those who excelled have nearly always been Germans. But where did they find fortune, where fame? Certainly not in Germany. Even Gluck;—did Germany make him a great man? Alas, no!

Vienna, August 17, 1782, to his father. Mozart's answer in 1789, when King Frederick William II of Prussia said to him: "Stay with me; I offer you a salary of 3,000 thalers," was touching in the extreme: "Shall I leave my good Emperor?" Thereupon the king said: "Think it over. I'll keep my word even if you should come after a year and a day!" In spite of his financial difficulties, Mozart never gave serious consideration to the offer. When his father advised him against some of his foreign plans he answered: "So far as France and England are concerned you are wholly right; this opening will never be closed to me; it will be better if I wait a while longer. Meanwhile it is possible that conditions may change in those countries." In a preceding letter he had written: "I have been exercising myself daily in the French language, and already taken three lessons in English. In three months I hope to be able to read and understand the English books fairly well."

118. The two of us played a sonata that I had composed for the occasion, and which had a success. This sonata I shall send you by Herr von Daubrawaick, who said that he would feel proud to have it in his trunk; his son, who is a Salzburger, told me this. When the father went he said, quite loud, "I am proud to be your countryman. You are doing great honor to Salzburg; I hope that times will so change that we can have you amongst us, and then do not forget me." I answered: "My fatherland has always the first claim on me."

Vienna, November 24, 1781, to his father. Mozart is speaking of a concert which he had given. The sonata is the small one in D major (Köchel, No. 381). Mozart often made merry over the Salzburgians; he called them stupid and envious.

119. Thoroughly convinced that I was talking to a German, I gave free rein to my tongue,—a thing which one is so seldom permitted to do that after such an outpouring of the heart it would be allowable to get a bit fuddled without risk of hurting one's health.

Vienna, March 21, 1785, to Anton Klein.

SELF-RESPECT AND HONOR

Beethoven is said to have been the first musician who compelled respect for his craft,—he who, prouder than Goethe, associated with royalties, and said of himself, "I, too, am a king!" Mozart rose from a dependent position which brought him most grievous humiliations; he was looked upon as a servant of the Archbishop of Salzburg, and treated accordingly. At the time composers and musicians had no higher standing. Mozart feels the intolerableness of his position and protests against it on every opportunity; he is conscious of his worth and intellectual superiority. When he endures the grossest indignities from his tormentor, Archbishop Hieronymus, it is for the sake of his father whom he would save from annoyance. In all things else he follows the example of his father, but in the matter of self-respect he admonishes and encourages his parent. Although Beethoven rudely rejected the condescending good will of the great which would have made Mozart happy, and demanded respect as an equal, it must be confessed that the generally manly conduct of Mozart was an excellent preparation of the Viennese soil.

120. I only wish that the Elector were here; he might hear something to his advantage. He knows nothing about me, knows nothing about my ability. What a pity that these grand gentlemen take everybody's word and are unwilling to investigate for themselves! It's always the way. I am willing to make a test; let him summon all the composers in Munich, and even invite a few from Italy, Germany, England and Spain; I will trust myself in a competition with them all.

49

Munich, October 2, 1777, to his father. Mozart had hoped to secure
an appointment in Munich, but was disappointed.

121. I could scarcely refrain from laughing when I was intro-
duced to the people. A few, who knew me *par renommée*, were
very polite and respectful; others who know nothing about me
stared at me as if they were a bit amused. They think that because I am small and young that there can be nothing great and
old in me. But they shall soon find out.

Mannheim, October 31, 1777, to his father.

122. We poor, common folk must not only take wives whom
we love and who love us, but we may, can and want to take such
because we are neither noble, well-born nor rich, but lowly,
mean and poor. Hence we do not need rich wives because our
wealth dies with us, being in our heads. Of this wealth no man
can rob us unless he cuts off our heads, in which case we should
have need of nothing more.

Mannheim, February 7, 1778, to his father. Mozart had fallen in love
with Aloysia, daughter of the poor musician Weber.

123. I will gladly give lessons to oblige, particularly if I see
that a person has talent and a joyous desire to learn. But to go
to a house at a fixed hour, or wait at home for the arrival of
some one, that I can not do, no matter how much it might yield
me; I leave that to others who can do nothing else than play the
clavier,—for me it is impossible. I am a composer and was born
to be a chapelmaster. I dare not thus bury the talent for composition which a kind God gave me in such generous measure (I
may say this without pride for I feel it now more than ever
before), and that is what I should do had I many pupils. Teach-
ing is a restless occupation and I would rather neglect clavier
playing than composition; the clavier is a side issue, though,
thank God, a strong one.

Mannheim, February 7, 1778, to his father, who must have read
the words with sorrow, since he and his daughter Nannerl were laboriously giving lessons and practising economy to make Mozart's journey
possible and had to advance money to him.

124. I know of a certainty that the Emperor intends to establish a German opera in Vienna, and is earnestly seeking a young conductor who understands the German language, has genius and is capable of giving the world something new. Benda of Gotha is seeking the place and Schweitzer is also an applicant. I believe this would be a good thing for me,—but with good pay, as a matter of course. If the Emperor will give me a thousand florins, I will write a German opera for him, and if then he does not wish to retain me, all right. I beg of you, write to all the good friends in Vienna whom you can think of that I would do honor to the Emperor. If there is no other way let him try me with an opera.

Mannheim, January 10, 1778, to his father.

125. The greatest favor that Herr Grimm showed me was to lend me 15 Louis d'Or in driblets at the (life and) death of my blessed mother. Is he fearful that the loan will not be returned? If so he truly deserves a kick—for he shows distrust of my honesty (the only thing that can throw me into a rage), and also of my talent. . . . In a word he belongs to the Italian party, is deceitful and is seeking to oppress me.

Paris, September 11, 1778, to his father, who was on a friendly footing with the French encyclopædist Grimm since the first artistic tour made with little Wolfgang in 1763, when he owed many favors to Grimm. Apparently Mozart here does an injustice to his patron, who, it is true, thought highly of the Italian Piccini.

126. On my honor, I can't help it; it's the kind of man I am. Lately when he spoke to me rudely, foolishly and stupidly, I did not dare to say to him that he need not worry about the 15 Louis d'Or for fear that I might offend *him*. I did nothing but endure and ask if he were ready; and then—your obedient servant.

Paris, September 11, 1778, to his father, at whose request Baron Grimm had received the young artist in Paris, but at the same time had exercised a sort of artistic guardianship over him. Wolfgang had written to his father as early as August 27: "If you write to him do not be too humble in your thanks;—there are reasons." On another occasion: "Grimm is able to assist children, but not adults. Do not imagine that he is the man he was."

127. You know that I want nothing more than good employment,—good in character and good in recompense, let it be where it will if the place be but Catholic . . . ; but if the Salzburgians want me they must satisfy my desires or they will certainly not get me.

Paris, July 3, 1778, to his father, who wished to see his son in the service of the Archiepiscopal court at Salzburg.

128. The Prince must have confidence either in you or me, and give us complete control of everything relating to music; otherwise all will be in vain. For in Salzburg everybody or nobody has to do with music. If I were to undertake it I should demand free hands. In matters musical the Head Court Chamberlain should have nothing to say; a cavalier can not be a conductor, but a conductor can well be a cavalier.

Paris, July 9, 1778.

129. If the Archbishop were to entrust it to me I would soon make his music famous, that's sure. . . . But I have one request to make at Salzburg, and that is that I shall not be placed among the violins where I used to be; I'll never make a fiddler. I will conduct at the clavier and accompany the arias. It would have been a good thing if I had secured a written assurance of the conductorship.

Paris, September 11, 1778, to his father who had urged him to return to Salzburg to receive an appointment to the conductorship. Mozart seems to have a premonition of the treatment which he received later from the Archbishop.

130. I must admit that I should reach Salzburg with a lighter heart if I were not aware that I have taken service there; it is only this thought that is intolerable. Put yourself in my place and think it over. At Salzburg I do not know who or what I am; I am everything and at times nothing. I do not demand too much or too little;—only something, if I am something.

Strassburg, October 15, 1778, to his father, while returning from Paris filled with repugnance to the Archbishop. "For aside from obeying a praiseworthy and beautiful motive" (he means filial affection), "I am really committing the greatest folly in the world," he writes in the same letter.

131. The Archbishop can not recompense me for the slavery in Salzburg! As I have said I experience great pleasure when I think of visiting you again, but nothing but vexation and fear at the thought of seeing myself at that beggarly court again. The Archbishop must not attempt to put on grand airs with me as he used to; it is not impossible, it is even likely that I would put my fingers to my nose,—and I know full well that you would enjoy it as much as I.

Mannheim, November 12, 1778, to his father.

132. At 11 o'clock in the forenoon, a little too early for me, unfortunately, we already go to table; we dine together,—the two temporal and spiritual valets, Mr. the Controller, Mr. Zetti, the Confectioner, Messrs. the two cooks, Ceccarelli, Brunetti and my insignificance. N.B. The two valets sit at the head of the table; I have at least the honor of sitting above the cooks. Well, I simply think I am at Salzburg. At dinner a great many coarse and silly jokes are cracked, but not at me, because I do not speak a word unless of necessity and then always with the utmost seriousness. As soon as I have dined I go my way.

Vienna, March 17, 1781, to his father. The Archbishop was visiting Vienna and had brought with him his best musicians whom, however, he treated shabbily. At length the rupture came; Mozart was dismissed —literally with a kick.

133. Believe me, best of fathers, that I must summon all my manhood to write to you what reason commands. God knows how hard it is for me to leave you; but if beggary were my lot I would no longer serve such a master; for that I shall never forget as long as I live,—and I beg of you, I beg of you for the sake of everything in the world, encourage me in my determination instead of trying to dissuade me. That would unfit me for what I

must do. For it is my desire and hope to win honor, fame and money, and I hope to be of greater service to you in Vienna than in Salzburg.

Vienna, May 12, 1781, to his father.

134. I did not know that I was a *valet de chambre*, and that broke my neck. I ought to have wasted a few hours every forenoon in the antechamber. I was often told that I should let myself be seen, but I could not recall that this was my duty and came punctually only when the Archbishop summoned me.

Vienna, May 12, 1781.

135. To please you, best of fathers, I would sacrifice my happiness, my health and my life; but my honor is my own, and ought to be above all else to you. Let Count Arco and all Salzburg read this letter.

Vienna, May 19, 1781. It was Count Arco who had dismissed Mozart with a kick. The father was thrown into consternation at the maltreatment of his son and sought to persuade Mozart to return to Salzburg. Mozart replied: "Best, dearest father, ask of me anything you please but not that; the very thought makes me tremble with rage."

136. You did not think when you wrote this that such a backstep would stamp me as one of the most contemptible fellows in the world. All Vienna knows that I have left the Archbishop, knows why, knows that it is because of my injured honor, of an injury inflicted three times,—and I am to make a public denial, proclaim myself a cur and the Archbishop a noble prince? No man could do the former, least of all I, and the second can only be done by God if He should choose to enlighten him.

Vienna, May 19, 1781, to his father, who had asked him to return to the service of the Archbishop.

137. If it be happiness to be rid of a prince who never pays one, but torments him to death, then I am happy. For if I had to work from morning till night I would do it gladly rather than live off the bounty of such a,—I do not dare to call him by the

name he deserves,—I was forced to take the step I did and I can not swerve a hair's breadth from it; impossible.

·Vienna, May 19, 1781.

138. Salzburg is nothing now to me except it offer an opportunity to give the Count a kick . . . even if it were in the public street. I desire no satisfaction from the Archbishop, for he is not in a position to offer me the kind that I want and must have. Within a day or two I shall write to the Count telling him what he can confidently expect to receive from me the first time I meet him, be it where it may, except a place that commands my respect.

Vienna, June 13, 1781, to his father. Count Arco's offence has been mentioned. On June 16 Mozart wrote: "The hungry ass shall not escape my chastisement if I have to wait twenty years; for as soon as I see him he shall come in contact with my foot, unless I should be so unfortunate as to see him in the sanctuary." [The reader will probably guess that the translator is resorting to euphemisms in rendering Mozart's language. H. E. K.]

139. It is the heart that confers the patent of nobility on man; and although I am no count I probably have more honor within me than many a count. Menial or count, whoever insults me is a cur. I shall begin by representing to him, with complete gravity, how badly he did his business, but at the end I shall have to assure him in writing that he is to expect a kick . . . and a box on the ear from me; for if a man insults me I have got to be revenged, and if I give him no more than he gave me, it is mere retaliation and not punishment. Besides I should thus put myself on a level with him, and I am too proud to compare myself with such a stupid gelding.

Vienna, June 20, 1781, to his father. These expressions, called out by the insulting treatment received from the Archbishop and Count Arco, are in striking contrast to Mozart's habitual amiability.

140. I can easily believe that the court parasites will look askance at you, but why need you disturb yourself about such a miserable pack? The more inimical such persons are to you the

greater the pride and contempt with which you should look down upon them.

Vienna, June 20, 1778, to his father, who fears that some of the consequences of his son's step may be visited upon him.

141. I do not ask of you that you make a disturbance or enter the least complaint, but the Archbishop and the whole pack must fear to speak to you about this matter, for you (if compelled) can without the slightest alarm say frankly that you would be ashamed to have reared a son who would have accepted abuse from such an infamous cur as Arco; and you may assure all that if I had the good luck to meet him to-day I should treat him as he deserves, and that he would have occasion to remember me the rest of his life. All that I want is that everybody shall see in your bearing that you have nothing to fear. Keep quiet; but if necessary, speak, and then to some purpose.

Vienna, July 4, 1781, to his father.

142. I may say that because of Vogler, Winter was always my greatest enemy. But because he is a beast in his mode of life, and in all other matters a child, I would be ashamed to set down a single word on his account; he deserves the contempt of all honorable men. I will, therefore, not tell infamous truths rather than infamous lies about him.

Vienna, December 22, 1781, to his father, to whose ears Peter Winter, a composer, had brought slanderous reports concerning Mozart and his Constanze. Winter was a pupil of Abbé Vogler. (See No. 66.)

143. He is a nice fellow and a good friend of mine; I might often dine with him, but it is a custom with me never to take pay for my favors; nor would a dish of soup pay them. Yet such people have wonderful notions of what they accomplish with one. . . . I am fond of doing favors for people but they must not plague me. She (the daughter) is not satisfied if I spend two hours every day with her, but wants me to loll about the whole day; yet she tries to play the well behaved one.

Vienna, August 22, 1781, to his father. Mozart is writing about a landlord and his daughter concerning whom favorable reports had reached the ears of the father. Mozart explains matters and soon thereafter announces a change of lodgings.

144. I beg of you that when you write to me about something in my conduct which is displeasing to you, and I in turn give you my views, let it always be a matter between father and son, and therefore a secret not to be divulged to others. Let our letters suffice and do not address yourself to others, for, by heaven, I will not give a finger's length of accounting concerning my doings or omissions to others, not even to the Emperor himself. I have cares and anxieties of my own and have no use for petulant letters.

Vienna, September 5, 1781, to his father, who lent a willing ear to gossips and was never chary of his reproaches. Mozart was already twenty-five years old.

145. If I were Wiedmer I would demand the following satisfaction from the Emperor: he should endure 50 strokes at the same place in my presence and then he should pay me 6,000 ducats. If I could not obtain this satisfaction I should take none, but thrust a dagger through his heart at the first opportunity. N.B. He has already had an offer of 3,000 ducats on condition that he does not come to Vienna, but permits the matter to drop. The people of Innsbruck say of Wiedmer: he who was scourged for our sake will also redeem us.

Vienna, August 8, 1781, to his father. Herr von Wiedmer was a nobleman and theatre director, who, without cause, had been sentenced to a whipping by the president, Count Wolkenstein, on the complaint of another nobleman. [Mozart's bloodthirstiness was probably due to memories of Arco's kick still rankling in his heart. It was only after long solicitation from his father that he abandoned his plan to send Arco the threatened letter. H. E. K.]

146. You perhaps already know that the *musico* Marquesi— *Marquesius di Milano*—was poisoned in Naples; but how! He was in love with a duchess and her real *amant* grew jealous and

sent three or four bravos to Marquesi and left him the choice of drinking poison or being massacred. He chose the poison. Being a timid Italian he died alone and left his gentlemen murderers to live in rest and peace. Had they come into my room, I would have taken a few of them with me into the other world, as long as some one had to die. Pity for so excellent a singer!

Munich, December 30, 1780, to his father. Mozart, on the whole, was one of the most peaceable men on earth, but he was not wanting in personal courage, and he could fly into transports of rage.

147. If you were to write also to Prince Zeil I should be glad. But short and good. Do not by any means crawl! That I can not endure.

Mannheim, December 10, 1777, to his father. Count Ferdinand von Zeil was Prince Bishop of Chimsee and favorably disposed towards Mozart, who was hoping for an appointment in Munich. "If he wants to do something he can; all Munich told me that." Nothing came of it.

148. Whoever judges me by such bagatelles is also a scamp!

Mozart wrote many occasional pieces for his friends, fitting them to the players' capacities. Mozart said that the publisher who bought some of these "bagatelles" and printed them without applying to him was a scamp (*Lump*), but took no proceedings against him.

149. Very well; then I shall earn nothing more, go hungry and the devil a bit will I care!

Mozart's answer to Hofmeister, the Leipsic publisher, who had said: "Write in a more popular style or I can neither print nor pay for anything of yours."

STRIVINGS AND LABORS

150. We live in this world only that we may go onward without ceasing, a peculiar help in this direction being that one enlightens the other by communicating his ideas; in the sciences and fine arts there is always more to learn.

Salzburg, September 7, 1776, to Padre Martini of Bologna, whose opinion he asks concerning a motet which the Archbishop of Salzburg had faulted.

151. I am just now reading "Telemachus;" I am in the second part.

Bologna, September 8, 1770, to his mother and sister.

152. Because you said yesterday that you could understand anything, and that I might write what I please in Latin, curiosity has led me to try you with some Latin lines. Have the kindness when you have solved the problem to send the result to me by the Hagenauer servant maid.

Cuperem scire, de qua causa, a quam plurimis adolescentibus otium usque adeo aestimetur, ut ipsi se nec verbis, nec verberibus ab hoc sinant abduci.

The Archiepiscopal concertmaster, aged 13, writes thus to a girl friend.

153. Since then I have exercised myself daily in the French language, and already taken three lessons in English. In three months I hope to be able to read and understand the English books fairly well.

Vienna, August 17, 1782, to his father. Mozart had given it out that he intended to go to Paris or London. Prince Kaunitz had said to Archduke Maximilian that men like Mozart lived but once in a hundred years, and should not be driven out of Germany. Mozart, however, writes to his father: "But I do not want to wait on charity; I find that, even if it were the Emperor, I am not dependent on his bounty."

154. I place my confidence in three friends, and they are strong and invincible friends, viz: God, your head and my head. True, our heads differ, but each is very good, serviceable, and useful in its genre, and in time I hope that my head will be as good as yours in the field in which now yours is superior.

Mannheim, February 28, 1778, to his father.

155. Believe me, I do not love idleness, but work. True it was difficult in Salzburg and cost me an effort and I could scarcely persuade myself. Why? Because I was not happy there. You must admit that, for me at least, there was not a pennyworth of entertainment in Salzburg. I do not want to associate with many and of the majority of the rest I am not fond. There is no encouragement for my talent! If I play, or one of my compositions is performed, the audience might as well consist of tables and chairs. . . . In Salzburg I sigh for a hundred amusements, and here for not one; to live in Vienna is amusement enough.

Vienna, May 26, 1781, to his father, who was concerned as to the progress making in Vienna.

156. I beg of you, best and dearest of fathers, do not write me any more letters of this kind,—I conjure you, for they serve no other purpose than to heat my head and disturb my heart and mood. And I, who must compose continually, need a clear head and quiet mood.

Vienna, June 9, 1781, to his father, who had reproached him because of his rupture with the Archbishop.

157. If there ever was a time when I was not thinking about marriage it is now. I wish for nothing less than a rich wife, and if I could make my fortune by marriage now I should perforce

have to wait, because I have very different things in my head. God did not give me my talent to put it a-dangle on a wife, and spend my young life in inactivity. I am just beginning life, and shall I embitter it myself? I have nothing against matrimony, but for me it would be an evil just now.

Vienna, July 25, 1781, to his father, who was solicitous lest he fall in love with one of the daughters in the Weber family with whom he was living. All manner of rumors had been carried to him. The father persuaded his son to seek other lodgings; but Constanze Weber eventually became Mozart's wife nevertheless.

158. This sort of composer can do nothing in this genre. He has no conception of what is wanted. Lord! if God had only given me such a place in the church and before such an orchestra!

A remark made in Leipsic, in 1789, in reference to a composer who was suited to comic opera work, but had received an appointment as Church composer. Mozart examined a mass of his and said: "It sounds all very well, but not in church." He then played it through with new words improvised by himself, such as (in the *Cum sancto spiritu*) "Stolen property, gentlemen, but no offence."

159. You see my intentions are good; but if you can't, you can't! I do not want to scribble, and therefore can not send you the whole symphony before next post day.

Vienna, July 31, 1782, to his father, who had asked for a symphony for the Hafner family in Salzburg.

160. I do not beg pardon; no! But I beg of Herr Bullinger that he himself apply to himself for pardon in my behalf, with the assurance that as soon as I can do so in quiet I shall write to him. Until now no such occasion has offered itself, for as soon as I know that in all likelihood I must leave a place I have no restful hour. And although I still have a modicum of hope, I am not at ease and shall not be until I know my status.

Mannheim, November 22, 1777, to his father. Abbé Bullinger was the most intimate friend that the Mozart family had in Salzburg. Mozart had been negligent in his correspondence.

161. To live well and to live happily are different things, and the latter would be impossible for me without witchcraft; it would have to be supernatural; and that is impossible for there are no witches now-a-days.

Paris, August 7, 1778, to his friend Bullinger, who had sought to persuade him to return to Salzburg.

162. The Duke de Chabot sat himself down beside me and listened attentively; and I—I forgot the cold, and the headache and played regardless of the wretched clavier as I play when I am in the mood. Give me the best clavier in Europe and at the same time hearers who understand nothing or want to understand nothing, and who do not feel what I play with me, and all my joy is gone.

Paris, May 1, 1778, to his father. The Duchess had behaved very haughtily and kept Mozart sitting in a cold room for a long time before the Duke came.

AT HOME AND ABROAD

163. I assure you that without travel we (at least men of the arts and sciences) are miserable creatures. A man of mediocre talent will remain mediocre whether he travel or not; but a man of superior talent (which I can not deny I am, without doing wrong) deteriorates if he remains continually in one place.

Paris, September 11, 1778, to his father, who had secured an appointment for him at Salzburg which he was loath to accept. He asked that the Archbishop permit him to travel once in two years. He feared that he "would find no congenial society" in Salzburg, where, moreover, music did not stand in large appreciation. Mozart's subsequent experiences were of the most pitiable character.

164. Write me, how is Mr. Canary? Does he still sing? Does he still pipe? Do you know why I am thinking of the canary? Because there is one in our anteroom that makes the same little sounds as ours.

Naples, May 19, 1770, to his sister. Mozart was very fond of animals. In a letter from Vienna to his sister on August 21, 1773, he writes: "How is Miss Bimbes? Please present all manner of compliments to her." "Miss Bimbes" was a dog. At another time he wrote a pathetic little poem on the death of a starling. While in the midst of the composition and rehearsal of "Idomeneo" he wrote to his father: "Give Pimperl [a dog] a pinch of Spanish snuff, a good wine-biscuit and three busses."

165. Because of my disposition which leans towards a quiet, domestic life rather than to boisterousness, and the fact that since my youth I have never given a thought to my linen, cloth-

63

ing or such things, I can think of nothing more necessary than a wife. I assure you that I frequently spend money unnecessarily because I am negligent of these things. I am convinced that I could get along better than I do now on the same income if I had a wife. How many unnecessary expenditures would be saved? Others are added, it is true, but you know in advance what they are and can adjust them;—in a word you lead a regulated life. In my opinion an unmarried man lives only half a life; that is my conviction and I can not help it. I have resolved the matter over and over in my mind and am of the same opinion still.

Vienna, December 15, 1781, to his father.

166. At present I have only one pupil. . . . I could have several if I were to lower my fee; but as soon as one does that one loses credit. My price is twelve lessons for six ducats, and I make it understood besides that I give the lessons as a favor. I would rather have three pupils who pay well than six who pay ill. I am writing this to you to prevent you from thinking that it is selfishness which prevents me from sending you more than thirty ducats.

Vienna, June 16, 1781, to his father. [In American money Mozart's fee is represented by $1.20 per lesson. H. E. K.]

167. I could not go about Vienna looking like a tramp, particularly just at this time. My linen was pitiable; no servant here has shirts of such coarse stuff as mine,—and that certainly is a frightful thing for a man. Consequently there were again expenditures. I had only one pupil; she suspended her lessons for three weeks, and I was again the loser. One must not throw one's self away here,—that is a first principle,—or one is ruined forever. The most audacious man wins the day.

Vienna, September 5, 1781, to his father, excusing himself for not having made remittances.

168. Resent anything and at once you receive smaller pay. Besides all this the Emperor is a skinflint. If the Emperor wants me

he ought to pay for me; the mere honor of being in his employ is not enough. If the Emperor were to offer me 1,000 florins and a count 2,000, I should present my compliments to the Emperor and go to the count,—assuming a guarantee, of course.

Vienna, April 10, 1782, to his father. Mozart was not too industrious in the pursuit of a court appointment, yet had reason to be hopeful. Near the end of his short life the appointment came from Joseph II, to whom Mozart had been too faithful.

169. I described my manner of life to my father only recently, and I will now repeat it to you. At six o'clock in the morning I am already done with my *friseur,* and at seven I am fully dressed. Thereupon I compose until nine o'clock. From nine to one I give lessons; then I eat unless I am a guest at places where they dine at two or even three o'clock,—as, for instance, to-day and to-morrow with Countess Zichy and Countess Thun. I can not work before five or six o'clock in the evening and I am often prevented even then by a concert; if not I write till nine. Then I go to my dear Constanze, where the delight of our meeting is generally embittered by the words of her mother;—hence my desire to free and save her as soon as possible. At half after ten or eleven I am again at home. Since (owing to the occasional concerts and the uncertainty as to whether or not I may be called out) I can not depend on having time for composition in the evening, I am in the habit (particularly when I come home early) of writing something before I go to bed. Frequently I forget myself and write till one o'clock,—then up again at six.

Vienna, February 13, 1782, to his sister Marianne—Nannerl, as he called her.

170. We do not go to bed before 12 o'clock and get up half after five or five, because nearly every day we take an early walk in the Augarten.

Vienna, May 26, 1784, to his father, to whom he complains of his maid-servant who came from Salzburg and who had written to the father that she was not permitted to sleep except between 11 and 6 o'clock.

171. Now as to my mode of life: As soon as you were gone I played two games of billiards with Herr von Mozart who wrote the opera for Schickaneder's theatre; then I sold my nag for fourteen ducats; then I had Joseph call my *primus* and bring a black coffee, to which I smoked a glorious pipe of tobacco. . . . At 5:30 I went out of the door and took my favorite promenade through the Glacis to the theatre. What do I see? What do I smell? It is the *primus* with the cutlet *Gusto!* I eat to your health. It has just struck 11 o'clock. Perhaps you are already asleep. Sh! sh! sh! I do not want to wake you.

Saturday, the 8th. You ought to have seen me yesterday at supper! I could not find the old dishes and therefore produced a set as white as snow-flowers and had the wax candelabra in front of me.

Vienna, October 7, 1791, to his wife, who was taking the waters at Baden. Mozart was fond of billiards and often played alone as on this occasion. He was careful of his health and had been advised by his physician to ride; but he could not acquire a taste for the exercise—hence the sale of his horse. The *primus* was his valet, a servant found in every Viennese household at the time. Out of the door through which he stepped on beginning his walk to the theatre his funeral procession passed two months later.

172. I have done more work during the ten days that I have lived here than in two months in any other lodgings; and if it were not that I am too often harassed by gloomy thoughts which I can dispel only by force, I could do still more, for I live pleasantly, comfortably and cheaply.

Vienna, June 27, 1788, to his friend Puchberg.

173. I have no conveniences for writing there [*i.e.* at Baden], and I want to avoid embarrassments as much as possible. Nothing is more enjoyable than a quiet life and to obtain that one must be industrious. I am glad to be that.

Vienna, October 8, 1791, to his wife at Baden. Mozart probably refers to work on his "Requiem." He says further: "If I had had nothing to do I would have gone with you to spend the week."

174. Now the babe against my will, yet with my consent, has been provided with a wet nurse. It was always my determination that, whether she was able to do so or not, my wife was not to suckle her child; but neither was the child to guzzle the milk of another woman. I want it brought up on water as I and my sister were, but. . . .

Vienna, June 8, 1783, to his father, the day after his first child was born. The "Dear, thick, fat little fellow" died soon after.

175. Young as I am, I never go to bed without thinking that possibly I may not be alive on the morrow; yet not one of the many persons who know me can say that I am morose or melancholy. For this happy disposition I thank my Creator daily, and wish with all my heart that it were shared by all my fellows.

Vienna, April 4, 1787, to his father, shortly before the latter's death. Mozart himself died when he was not quite thirty-six years old.

176. If it chances to be convenient I shall call on the Fischers for a moment; longer than that I could not endure their warm room and the wine at table. I know very well that people of their class think they are bestowing the highest honors when they offer these things, but I am not fond of such things,—still less of such people.

Vienna, December 22, 1781, to his sister. Mozart was acquainted with the Fischer family from the time of his first journeys as a child. The contrast which he draws between the artist and the comfort-loving, commonplace citizen is diverting.

177. The Viennese are a people who soon grow weary and listless,—but only of the theatre. My *forte* is too popular to be neglected. This, surely, is Clavierland!

Spoken to Count Arco who had warned him against removing to Vienna because of the fickleness of the Viennese public. He wanted him to return to Salzburg.

178. I am writing at a place called Reisenberg which is an hour's distance from Vienna. I once stayed here over night; now

I shall remain a few days. The house is insignificant, but the surroundings, the woods in which a grotto has been built as natural as can be, are splendid and very pleasant.

Vienna, July 13, 1781, to his father. Like Beethoven, Mozart loved nature and wanted a garden about his home.

179. I wish that my sister were here in Rome. I am sure she would be pleased with the city, for St. Peter's church is regular, and many other things in Rome are regular.

Rome, April 14, 1770. A droll criticism from the traveling virtuoso, aged 14, in a letter to his mother and sister.

180. Carefully thinking it over I conclude that in no country have I received so many honors or been so highly appreciated as in Italy. You get credit in Italy if you have written an opera,—especially in Naples.

Munich, October 11, 1777, to his father. An influential friend had offered to help him get an appointment in Italy.

181. Strassburg can't get along without me. You have no idea how I am honored and loved here. The people say that everything I do is refined, that I am so sedate and courteous and have so good a bearing. Everybody knows me.

Strassburg, October 26, 1778, to his father, on his return journey from Paris. On October 3 he had written: "I beg your pardon if I cannot write much. It is because, unless I am in a city in which I am well known, I am never in a good humor. If I were acquainted here I would gladly stay, for the city is truly charming—beautiful houses, handsome broad streets, and superb squares."

182. Oh, what a difference between the people of the Palatinate and of Bavaria! What a language! How coarse! To say nothing of the mode of life!

Mannheim, November 12, 1778, to his father. Mozart, while returning from Paris, had stopped at his "dear Mannheim," where at the moment a regiment of Bavarian soldiers were quartered, and had just got news of the rudeness with which the people of Munich had treated their Elector.

183. In Regensburg we dined magnificently at noon, listened to divine table music, had angelic service and glorious Mosel wine. We breakfasted in Nuremberg,—a hideous city. At Würzburg we strengthened our stomachs with coffee; a beautiful, a splendid city. The charges were moderate everywhere. Only two post relays from here, in Aschaffenburg, the landlord swindled us shamefully.

Frankfort-on-the-Main, September 29, 1790, to his wife. The remark is notable because of the judgments pronounced on the renaissance city Nuremberg, and the rococo city Würzburg.

184. All the talk about the imperial cities is mere boasting. I am famous, admired and loved here, it is true, but the people are worse than the Viennese in their parsimony.

Mozart went to Frankfort, in 1790, on the occasion of the coronation of the emperor, hoping to make enough money with concerts to help himself out of financial difficulties, but failed.

LOVE AND FRIENDSHIP

Mozart's love for his father made him dependent on the latter to the end of his days. He was a model son and must have loved his wife devotedly, since, for her sake, he once in his life disobeyed his father. The majority of his letters which have been preserved are addressed to his father, to whom he reported all his happenings and whose advice he is forever seeking. Similar were his relations with his sister Marianne (Nannerl), whom he loved with great tenderness. The letters to his wife are unique; all of them, even the last, seem to be the letters of a lover. They were a pair of turtle-doves.

Mozart was an ideal friend, ready to sacrifice to the uttermost on the altar of friendship. It was this trait of character which made him throw himself with enthusiasm into Freemasonry, whose affiliations he sought to widen by drafting the constitution of a community which he called "The Grotto." He probably hated only one man in the world,—the Archbishop of Salzburg, his tormentor.

185. The moment you do not trust me I shall distrust myself. The time is past, it is true, when I used to stand on the settle, sing *oragna fiagata fà* and kiss the tip end of your nose; but have I therefore shown laxity in respect, love and obedience? I say no more.

Mannheim, February 19, 1779, to his father, who was vexed because Mozart was showing a disposition to stay in Mannheim, because of a love affair, instead of going to Paris. "Off with you to Paris, and soon!" wrote the father. The Italian words are meaningless and but a bit of child's play, the nature of which can be gathered from Mozart's remark.

186. Pray do not let your mind often harbor the thought that I shall ever forget you! It is intolerable to me. My chief aim in life has been, is, and will be to strive so that we may soon be reunited and happy. . . . Reflect that you have a son who will never consciously forget his filial duty toward you, and who will labor ever to grow more worthy of so good a father.

Mannheim, February 28, 1778, to his father.

187. The first thing I did after reading your letter was to go on my knees, and, out of a full heart, thank my dear God for this mercy. Now I am again at peace, since I know that I need no longer be concerned about the two persons who are the dearest things on earth to me.

Paris, July 31, 1778, to his father, who had written that he and Nannerl had comforted each other on the death of his mother.

188. Dearest, best of fathers! I wish you all conceivable good; whatever can be wished, that I wish you,—but no, I wish you nothing, but myself everything. For myself, then, I wish that you remain well and live innumerable years to my great happiness and pleasure; I wish that everything that I undertake may agree with your desire and liking,—or, rather, that I may undertake nothing which might not turn out to your joy. This also I hope, for whatever adds to the happiness of your son must naturally be agreeable also to you.

Vienna, November 16, 1781, to his father, congratulating him on his name-day. On March 17, 1778, Mozart had written from Mannheim: "Your accuracy extends to all things. 'Papa comes directly after God' was my maxim as a child and I shall stick to it."

189. Our little cousin is pretty, sensible, amiable, clever and merry, all because she has been in society; she visited Munich for a while. You are right, we suit each other admirably, for she, too, is a bit naughty. We play great pranks on the people hereabouts.

Augsburg, October 17, 1777, to his father. The "little cousin" was two years younger than Mozart. Her father was a master bookbinder

in Augsburg. The maiden seems later to have had serious designs on
the composer.

190. I shall be right glad when I meet a place in which there
is a court. I tell you that if I did not have so fine a Mr. Cousin
and Miss Cousin and so dear a little cousin, my regrets that I am
in Augsburg would be as numerous as the hairs of my head.

Augsburg, October 17, 1777, to his father, whose birthplace he was
visiting on a concert tour. Mozart was vexed at the insolence of the
patricians.

191. In the case of Frau Lange I was a fool,—that's certain; but
what is a fellow not when he's in love? I did really love her, and
am not indifferent toward her even now. It's lucky for me that
her husband is a jealous fool and never permits her to go anywhere, so that I seldom see her.

Vienna, May 12, 1781, to his father, at the time when he was being
outrageously treated by the Archbishop. Frau Lange was Aloysia Weber,
sister of Constanze, to whom Mozart transferred his love and whom he
made his wife. Aloysia married an actor at the Court Theatre, Josef
Lange, with whom she lived unhappily.

192. I will not say that when at the house of the Mademoiselle
to whom I seem already to have been married off, I am morose
and silent; but neither am I in love. I jest with her and amuse
her when I have time (which is only evenings when I sup at
home, for in the forenoons I write in my room and in the after-
noons I am seldom at home); only that and nothing more. If I
were obliged to marry all the girls with whom I have jested I
should have at least 200 wives.

Vienna, July 25, 1781, to his father, who had heard all manner of
tales concerning the relations of Mozart and Constanze Weber.

193. My good, dear Constanze is the martyr, and, perhaps for
that very reason, the best hearted, cleverest, and (in a word) the
best of them all. She assumes all the cares of the house and yet
does not seem able to accomplish anything. O, best of fathers, I
could write pages if I were to tell you all the scenes that have

taken place in this house because of us two. . . . Constanze is not
ugly, but anything but beautiful; all her beauty consists of two
little black eyes and a handsome figure. She is not witty but has
enough common sense to be able to perform her duties as wife
and mother. She is not inclined to finery,—that is utterly false;
on the contrary, she is generally ill clad, for the little that the
mother was able to do for her children was done for the other
two—nothing for her. True, she likes to be neatly and cleanly,
though not extravagantly, dressed, and she can herself make most
of the clothes that a woman needs; she also dresses her own hair
every day, understands housekeeping, has the best heart in the
world,—tell me, could I wish a better wife?

Vienna, December 15, 1781, to his father. Constanze seems to have
been made for Mozart; they went through the years of their brief wed-
ded life like two children.

194. Dearest, best of friends!

Surely you will let me call you that? You can not hate me so
greatly as not to permit me to be your friend, and yourself to
become mine? And even if you do not want to be my friend
longer, you can not forbid me to think kindly of you as I have
been in the habit of doing. Consider well what you said to me
to-day. Despite my entreaties you gave me the mitten three times
and told me to my face that you would have nothing further to
do with me. I, to whom it is not such a matter of indifference as
it is to you to lose a sweetheart, am not so hot tempered, incon-
siderate or unwise as to accept that mitten. I love you too dearly
for that. I therefore beg you to ponder on the cause of your in-
dignation. A little confession of your thoughtless conduct would
have made all well,—if you do not take it ill, dear friend, may
still make all well. From this you see how much I love you. I do
not flare up as you do; I think, I consider, and I feel. If you have
any feeling I am sure that I will be able to say to myself before
night: Constanze is the virtuous, honor-loving, sensible and faithful sweetheart of just and well-meaning Mozart.

Vienna, April 29, 1782, to his fiancée, Constanze Weber. She had
played at a game of forfeits such as was looked upon lightly by the
frivolous society of the period in Vienna. Mozart rebuked her and she

broke off the engagement. The letter followed and soon thereafter a reconciliation. Mozart had said to her: "No girl who is jealous of her honor would do such a thing."

195. She is an honest, good girl of decent parents;—I am able to provide her with bread;—we love each other and want each other! . . . It is better to put one's things to rights and be an honest fellow!—God will give the reward! I do not want to have anything to reproach myself with.

Vienna, July 31, 1782, to his father, who had given his consent, hesitatingly and unwillingly, to the marriage of his son who was twenty-six years old. On August 7 Mozart wrote to him: "I kiss your hands and thank you with all the tenderness which a son should feel for his father, for your kind permission and paternal blessing."

196. If I were to tell you all the things that I do with your portrait, you would laugh heartily. For instance when I take it out of its prison house I say "God bless you, Stanzerl! God bless you, you little rascal,—*Krallerballer*—Sharpnose—little Bagatelle!" And when I put it back I let it slip down slowly and gradually and say "Nu,—Nu,—Nu,—Nu;" but with the emphasis which this highly significant word demands, and at the last, quickly: "Good-night, little Mouse, sleep well!" Now, I suppose, I have written down a lot of nonsense (at least so the world would think); but for us, who love each other so tenderly, it isn't altogether silly.

Dresden, April 13, 1789, to his wife in Vienna.

197. Dear little wife, I have a multitude of requests; *1mo,* I beg of you not to be sad.

2do, that you take care of your health and not trust the spring air.

3tio, that you refrain from walking out alone, or, better, do not walk out at all.

4to, that you rest assured of my love. Not a letter have I written to you but that your portrait was placed in front of mine.

5to, I beg of you to consider not only my honor and yours in your conduct but also in appearances. Do not get angry because of this request. You ought to love me all the more because I make so much of honor.

Dresden, April 16, 1789, to his wife, in Vienna, who was fond of life's pleasures.

198. You can not imagine how slowly time goes when you are not with me! I can't describe the feeling; there is a sort of sense of emptiness, which hurts—a certain longing which can not be satisfied, and hence never ends, but grows day by day. When I remember how childishly merry we were in Baden, and what mournful, tedious hours I pass here, my work gives me no pleasure, because it is not possible as was my wont, to chat a few words with you when stopping for a moment. If I go to the *Clavier* and sing something from the opera ["Die Zauberflöte"] I must stop at once because of my emotions.—*Basta!*

Vienna, July 7, 1791, to his wife, who was taking the waters at Baden.

199. I call only him or her a friend who is a friend under all circumstances, who thinks day or night of nothing else than to promote the welfare of a friend, who urges all well-to-do friends and works himself to make the other person happy.

Kaisersheim, December 18, 1778, to his father. Mozart was making the journey from Mannheim to Munich in the carriage of a prelate. The parting with his Mannheim friends, especially with Frau Cannabich, his motherly friend, was hard. "For me, who never made a more painful parting than this, the journey was only half pleasant—it would even have been a bore, if from childhood I had not been accustomed to leave people, countries and cities."

200. Permit me to beg for a continuance of your precious friendship, and to ask you to accept mine for now and forever; with an honest heart I vow it to you everlastingly. True, it will be of little use to you; but it will be the more durable and honest for that reason. You know that the best and truest friends are the poor. Rich people know nothing of friendship!—especially those who are born rich and those who have become rich fortuitously, —they are too often wrapped up completely in their own luck!

But there is nothing to fear from a man who has been placed in advantageous circumstances, not through blind, but deserved good fortune, through merit,—a man who did not lose courage because of his first failures,—who remained true to his religion and trust in God, was a good Christian and an honest man and cherished and valued his true friend,—in a word,—a man who has deserved better fortune—from such a man, there is nothing to fear.

Paris, August 7, 1778, to his friend Bullinger, in Salzburg, to whom he felt beholden for the gentle and considerate way in which he had broken the news of his mother's death to the family.

$201.$ My friend, had I but the money which many a man who does not deserve it wastes so miserably,—if I only had it! O, with what joy would I not help you!—But, alas! those who can will not, and those who would like to can not!

Paris, July 29, 1778, to Fridolin Weber, father of Constanze. The letter was found but recently among some Goethe autographs.

WORLDLY WISDOM

Mozart's father brought him up to be worldly wise. While journeying at a tender age through the world with his father the lad became an eye witness of the paternal business management with all its attention to detail; of the art of utilizing persons and conditions in order to achieve material results. As a youth he repeats the journeys accompanied by his mother, whom he loses by death in Paris. Regularly from Salzburg his father sends him letters full of admonitions and advice, the subjects almost systematically grouped. The worldly wisdom of the son is the fruit of paternal education, which he did not outgrow up to the day of his death. But life, experience, was also an educator; a seeming distrust of mankind speaks out of many a passage in his letters, but on the whole he thought too well of his fellowmen, and remained blind to the faults of his false friends who basely exploited him for their own ends. Although gifted with keen powers of observation, he always followed his kind heart instead of his better judgment and his sister spoke no more than the truth when she said after his death: "Outside of music he was, and remained, nearly always, a child. This was the chief trait of his character on its shady side; he always needed a father, mother, or other guardian."

202. Reflect, too, on this only too certain truth: it is not always wise to do all the things contemplated. Often one thinks one thing would be most advisable and another unadvisable and bad, when, if it were done, the opposite results would disclose themselves.

Mannheim, December 10, 1777, to his father, when a plan for an appointment in Mannheim came to naught.

203. I am not indifferent but only resolved, and therefore, I can endure everything with patience,—provided, only, that neither my honor nor the good name of Mozart shall suffer therefrom. Well, since it must be so, so be it; only I beg, do not rejoice or sorrow prematurely; for let happen what may, it will be all right so long as we remain well—happiness exists only in the imagination.

Mannheim, November 29, 1777, to his father, who had upbraided him because of his reckless expenditures. At the time Mozart was hoping for an appointment at Mannheim.

204. Dearest and best of fathers:—You shall see that things go better and better with me. What use is this perpetual turmoil, this hurried fortune? It does not endure.—*Chi va piano va sano.* One must adjust himself to circumstances.

Vienna, December 22, 1781, to his father, just before Mozart's marriage engagement to Constanze Weber.

205. Now, to put your mind at ease, I am doing nothing without reasons, and well-founded ones, too.

Vienna, October 21, 1781, to his "little cousin," who may still have cherished hopes of capturing her merry kinsman.

206. I have no news except that 35, 59, 60, 61, 62, were the winning numbers in the lottery, and, therefore, that if we had played those numbers we would have won; but that inasmuch as we did not play those numbers we neither won nor lost but had a good laugh at others.

Milan, October 26, 1771, to his sister.

207. Everybody was extremely courteous, and therefore I was also very courteous; for it is my custom to conduct myself towards others as they conduct themselves towards me,—it's the best way to get along.

Augsburg, October 14, 1777, to his father.

208. In Vienna and all the imperial hereditaments the theatres will all open in six weeks. It is wisely designed; for the dead are not so much benefited by the long mourning as many people are harmed.

Munich, December 13, 1780, to his father. Empress Maria Theresa had died on November 29. Mozart had greatly revered her from his youth. Nevertheless, he takes a practical view of the situation since the production of his opera "Idomeneo" is imminent. He requests of his father to have his "black coat thoroughly dusted, cleaned and put to rights," and to send it to him, since "everybody would go into mourning, and I, who will be summoned hither and thither, must weep along with the others."

209. Rest assured that I am a changed man; outside of my health I know of nothing more necessary than money. I am certainly not a miser,—it would be difficult for me to change myself into one—and yet the people here think me more disposed to be stingy than prodigal; and for a beginning that will suffice. So far as pupils are concerned I can have as many as I want; but I do not want many; I want better pay than the others, and therefore I am content with fewer. One must put on a few airs at the beginning or one is lost, *i.e.* one must travel the common road with the many.

Vienna, May 26, 1781, to his father.

210. Depend confidently on me. I am no longer a fool, and you will still less believe that I am a wicked and ungrateful son. Meanwhile trust my brains and my good heart implicitly, and you shall never be sorry. How should I have learned to value money? I never had enough of it in my hands. I remember that once when I had 20 ducats I thought myself rich. Need alone teaches the value of money.

Vienna, May 26, 1781, to his father.

211. If it were possible that it should vex me I should do my best not to notice it; as it is, thank God, there is no need of my deceiving myself because only the opposite could vex me, and I

should have had to decline, which is always too bad when one is dealing with a grand gentleman.

Vienna, October 5, 1782, to his father. Mozart had expected to give music lessons to a princess, but another teacher was chosen. Continuing in the same letter, he says: "I need only tell you his fee and you will easily be able to judge from it the strength of the master—400 florins. His name is Summerer."

212. I shall compose an opera but not in order, for the sake of 100 ducats, to see the theatre earn four times as much in a fortnight. I shall perform my opera at my own cost and make at least 1,200 florins in three performances; then the director can have the work for 50 ducats. If he does not want it I shall have received my pay and can utilize the opera elsewhere. I hope that you have never observed a tendency to dishonest dealing in me. One ought not to be a bad fellow, but neither ought one to be a stupid who is willing to let others benefit from the work which cost him study, care and labor, and surrender all claims for the future.

Vienna, October 5, 1782, to his father. Mozart's plans for exploiting his opera were never realized.

213. Yesterday I dined with the Countess Thun, and to-morrow I shall dine with her again. I let her hear all that was complete; she told me that she would wager her life that everything that I have written up to date would please. In such matters I care nothing for the praise or censure of anybody until the whole work has been seen or heard; instead I follow my own judgment and feelings.

Vienna, August 8, 1781, to his father. The opera in question was "Die Entführung aus dem Serail."

214. Magnanimity and gentleness have often reconciled the worst enemies.

Vienna, July 8, 1791, to his wife, who had somewhat rudely repulsed the advances of one of the visitors at Baden where she was taking the waters.

IN SUFFERING

It is as difficult to call up in the fancy a picture of a suffering Mozart as a merry Beethoven. The effect of melancholy hours is scarcely to be found in Mozart's music. When he composed,—*i.e.* according to his own expression "speculated" while walking up and down, revolving musical ideas in his mind and forming them into orderly compositions, so that the subsequent transcription was a mechanical occupation which required but little effort,— he was transported to the realm of tones, far from the miseries of this world. Nor would his happy disposition permit him long to remain under the influence of grief and care. None of the letters which sound notes of despair lacks a jest in which the writer forcibly tears himself away from his gloomy thoughts. His sufferings came to him from without; the fate of a Beethoven was spared him. Others brought him pain,—his rivals through envy, the Archbishop through malevolence, the Emperor through ignorance. Sufferings of this character challenged opposition and called out his powers, presenting to us a Mozart full of temperament and capable of measuring himself with any opponent.

He never lost hope even when hope seemed most deceptive. It is therefore impossible to speak of a suffering Mozart in the sense that we speak of a suffering Beethoven; fate was kind even at his death, which was preceded by but a brief illness.

215. I am still full of gall! . . . Three times this—I do not know what to call him—has assailed me to my face with impertinence and abuse of a kind that I did not want to write down, my best of fathers, and I did not immediately avenge the insult because

I thought of you. He called me a wretch (*Buben*), a licentious fellow, told me to get out and I—suffered it all, feeling that not only my honor but yours as well was attacked; but,—it was your wish,—I held my tongue.

Vienna, May 9, 1781, to his father, who had heard with deep concern of the treatment which his son was enduring at the hands of the Archbishop of Salzburg, and who feared for his own position. At the close of the letter Mozart writes: "I want to hear nothing more about Salzburg; I hate the Archbishop to the verge of madness."

216. The edifying things which the Archbishop said to me in the three audiences, particularly in the last, and what I have again been told by this glorious man of God, had so admirable a physical effect on me that I had to leave the opera in the evening in the middle of the first act, go home, and to bed. I was in a fever, my whole body trembled, and I reeled like a drunken man in the street. The next day, yesterday, I remained at home and all forenoon in bed because I had taken the tamarind water.

Vienna, May 12, 1781, to his father. The catastrophe between Mozart and the Archbishop is approaching.

217. Twice the Archbishop gave me the grossest impertinences and I answered not a word; more, I played for him with the same zeal as if nothing had happened. Instead of recognizing the honesty of my service and my desire to please him at the moment when I was expecting something very different, he begins a third tirade in the most despicable manner in the world.

Vienna, June 13, 1781, to his father. See the chapter "Self-Respect and Honor."

218. All the world asserts that by my braggadocio and criticisms I have made enemies of the professional musicians! Which world? Presumably that of Salzburg, for anybody living in Vienna sees and hears differently; there is my answer.

Vienna, July 31, to his father, who had sent Mozart what the latter called "so indifferent and cold a letter," when informed by his son of the great success of his opera, "Die Entführung aus dem Serail." As on previous occasions Salzburg talebearers had been busying themselves.

219. I rejoice like a child at the prospect of being with you again. I should have to be ashamed of myself if people could look into my heart; so far as I am concerned it is cold,—cold as ice. Yes, if you were with me I might find greater pleasure in the courteous treatment which I receive from the people; but as it is, it is all empty. Adieu!—Love!

Frankfort, September 30, 1790, to his wife. Mozart had made the journey to Frankfort to give concerts amidst the festivities accompanying the coronation of Leopold II, hoping that he could better his financial condition. Not having been sent at the cost of the Emperor, like other Court musicians, he pawned his silver, bought a carriage and took with him his brother-in-law, a violinist named Hofer. "It took us only six days to make the journey." He was disappointed in his expectations. "I have now decided to do as well as I can here and look joyfully towards a meeting with you. What a glorious life we shall lead; I shall work—work!"

220. Dreams give me no concern, for there is no mortal man on earth who does not sometimes dream. But merry dreams! quiet, refreshing, sweet dreams! Those are the thing! Dreams which, if they were realities, would make tolerable my life which has more of sadness in it than merriment.

Munich, December 31, 1778, to his father. During Mozart's sojourn in Paris the love of Aloysia Weber had grown cold, and Mozart was in the dolors.

221. Happy man! Now see,—I have got to give still another lesson in order to earn some money.

1786, to Gyrowetz, on the latter's departure for Italy.

222. You can not doubt my honesty, for you know me too well for that. Nor can you be suspicious of my words, my conduct or my mode of life, because you know my conduct and mode of life. Therefore,—forgive my confidence in you,—I am still very unhappy,—always between fear and hope.

Vienna, July 17, 1788, to his faithful friend, Puchberg, whom he has asked for money on account of the severe illness of his wife.

223. You know my circumstances;—to be brief, since I can not find a true friend, I am obliged to borrow money from usurers. But as it takes time to hunt among these un-Christian persons for those who are the most Christian and to find them, I am so stripped that I must beg you, dear friend, for God's sake to help me out with what you can spare.

One of many requests for help sent to Puchberg. It was sent in 1790 and the original bears an endorsement: "May 17, sent 150 florins."

224. If you, worthy brother, do not help me out of my present predicament I shall lose my credit and honor, the only things which I care now to preserve.

Vienna, June 27, 1788, to Puchberg, who had sent him 200 florins ten days before. Puchberg was a brother Mason.

225. How I felt then! How I felt then! Such things will never return. Now we are sunk in the emptiness of everyday life.

Remarked on remembering that at the age of fourteen he had composed a "Requiem" at the command of Empress Maria Theresa and had conducted it as Chapelmaster of the imperial orchestra.

226. Did I not tell you that I was composing this "Requiem" for myself?

Said on the day of his death while still working on the "Requiem" for which he had received so mysterious a commission. The work had been ordered by a Count Walsegg, who made pretensions to musical composition, and who wished to palm it off as a work of his own, written in memory of his wife. Mozart never knew him.

227. I shall not last much longer. I am sure that I have been poisoned! I can not rid myself of this thought.

Mozart believed that he had been poisoned by one of his Italian rivals, his suspicion falling most strongly on Salieri. ["As regards Mozart, Salieri cannot escape censure, for though the accusation of having been the cause of his death has been long ago disproved, it is more than possible that he was not displeased at the removal of so formidable a rival. At any rate, though he had it in his power to influence the

Emperor in Mozart's favor, he not only neglected to do so, but even intrigued against him, as Mozart himself relates in a letter to his friend Puchberg. After his death, however, Salieri befriended his son, and gave him a testimonial which secured him his first appointment." C. F. Pohl, in "Grove's Dictionary of Music and Musicians."]

228. Stay with me to-night; you must see me die. I have long had the taste of death on my tongue, I smell death, and who will stand by my Constanze, if you do not stay?

Reported by his sister-in-law, Sophie, sister of Constanze.

229. And now I must go just as it had become possible for me to live quietly. Now I must leave my art just as I had freed myself from the slavery of fashion, had broken the bonds of speculators, and won the privilege of following my own feelings and composing freely and independently whatever my heart prompted! I must away from my family, from my poor children in the moment when I should have been able better to care for their welfare!

Uttered on his death-bed.

MORALS

As regards his manner of life and morals Mozart long stood in a bad light before the world. The slanderous stories all came from his enemies in Vienna, and a long time passed before their true character was recognized. A great contribution to this end was made by the publication of his letters, which disclose an extraordinarily strong moral sense. The tale of an alleged *liaison* with a certain Frau Hofdämel, as a result of which the deceived husband was said to have committed suicide, has been proved to be wholly untrue and without warrant.

It may be said, indeed, that Mozart was an exception among the men of his period. The immorality of the Viennese was proverbial. Karoline Pichler, a contemporary, writes as follows in her book of recollections of the eighth decade of the eighteenth century: "In Vienna at the time there reigned a spirit of appreciation for merriment and a susceptibility for every form of beauty and sensuous pleasure. There was the greatest freedom of thought and opinion; anything could be written and printed which was not, in the strictest sense of the words, contrary to religion and the state. Little thought was bestowed on good morals. There was considerable license in the current plays and novels. Kotzebue created a tremendous sensation. His plays . . . and a multitude of romances and tales (Meissner's sketches among other things) were all based on meretricious relations. All the world and every young girl read them without suspicion or offence. More than once had I read and seen these things; 'Oberon' was well known to me; so was Meissner's 'Alcibiades.' No mother hesitated to acquaint her daughter with such works and before our eyes there were so many living exemplars whose irregular conduct was notorious, that no mother could have kept her daughter in ignorance had she tried."

Mozart was a passionate jester and his jokes were coarse enough; of that there is no doubt. But these things were innocent at the time. The letters of the lad to his little cousin in Augsburg contain many passages that would be called of questionable propriety now; but the little cousin does not seem to have even blushed. The best witness to the morality of Mozart's life is his wife, who, after his death, wrote to the publishing firm of Breitkopf and Härtel: "His letters are beyond doubt the best criterion for his mode of thought, his peculiarities and his education. Admirably characteristic is his extraordinary love for me, which breathes through all his letters. Those of his last year on earth are just as tender as those which he must have written in the first year of our married life;—is it not so? I beg as a particular favor that special attention be called to this fact for the sake of his honor."

He was a Freemason with all his heart, and gave expression to his humanitarian feeling in his opera "The Magic Flute." Without suspicion himself, he thought everybody else good, which led to painful experiences with some of his friends.

230. Parents strive to place their children in a position which shall enable them to earn their own living; and this they owe to their children and the state. The greater the talents with which the children have been endowed by God, the more are they bound to make use of those talents to improve the conditions of themselves and their parents, to aid their parents and to care for their own present and future welfare. We are taught thus to trade with our talents in the Gospels. I owe it, therefore, to God and my conscience to pay the highest gratitude to my father, who tirelessly devoted all his hours to my education, and to lighten his burdens.

From his request for dismissal from service in August, 1777. He wished to undertake an artistic tour with his father. He received his dismissal from the Archbishop of Salzburg, who granted it right unwillingly, however.

231. Only one thing vexed me a trifle,—the question whether I had forgotten confession. I have no complaint to make, but I do ask one favor, and that is that you do not think so ill of me! I am fond of merriment, but, believe me, I can also be serious. Since I left Salzburg (and while still in Salzburg) I have met persons whose conduct was such that I would have been ashamed to talk and act as they did though they were ten, twenty or thirty years older than I! Again I humbly beg of you to have a better opinion of me.

Mannheim, December 20, 1777, to his father, in answer to a letter of reproaches.

232. With all my heart I do wish Herr von Schiedenhofen joy. It is another marriage for money and nothing else. I should not like to marry thus; I want to make my wife happy,—not have her make my fortune. For that reason I shall not marry but enjoy my golden freedom until I am so situated that I can support wife and children. It was necessary that Herr Sch. should marry a rich woman; that's the consequence of being a nobleman. The nobility must never marry from inclination or love, but only from considerations of interest, and all manner of side considerations. Nor would it be becoming in such persons if they were still to love their wives after the latter had done their duty and brought forth a plump heir.

Mannheim, February 7, 1778, to his father.

233. In my opinion there is nothing more shameful than to deceive an honest girl.

Paris, July 18, 1778, to his father.

234. I am unconscious of any guilt for which I might fear your reproaches. I have committed no error (meaning by error any act unbecoming to a Christian and an honest man). I am anticipating the pleasantest and happiest days, but only in company with you and my dearest sister. I swear to you on my honor that I can not endure Salzburg and its citizens (I speak of the natives). Their speech and mode of life are utterly intolerable.

Munich, January 8, 1779, to his father, who was urging his return
from Paris to take the post of Chapelmaster in Salzburg. The musicians
of Salzburg were notorious because of their loose lives.

235. From the way in which my last letter was received I observe to my sorrow that (just as if I were an arch scoundrel or
an ass, or both at once) you trust the tittle-tattle and scribblings
of other people more than you do me. But I assure you that this
does not give me the least concern. The people may write the
eyes out of their heads, and you may applaud them as much as
you please, it will not cause me to change a hair's breadth; I
shall remain the same honest fellow that I have always been.

Vienna, September 5, 1781, to his father, who was still listening to
the slander mongers. Mozart could not lightly forget the fact that it
was due to these gentlemen that he had been forced to leave the house
of the widow Weber with whose daughter Constanze he was in love.

236. You have been deceived in your son if you could believe
him capable of doing a mean thing. . . . You know that I could
not have acted otherwise without outraging my conscience and
my honor. . . . I beg pardon for my too hasty trust in your paternal love. Through this frank confession you have a new proof
of my love of truth and detestation of a lie.

Vienna, August 7, 1782, to his father, whose consent to his son's marriage did not arrive till the day after.

237. Dearest and best of fathers:—I beg of you, for the sake of
all that is good in the world, give your consent to my marriage
with my dear Constanze. Do not think that it is alone because
of my desire to get married; I could well wait. But I see that it
is absolutely essential to my honor, the honor of my sweetheart,
to my health and frame of mind. My heart is ill at ease, my mind
disturbed;—then how shall I do any sensible thinking or work?
Why is this? Most people think we are already married; this
enrages the mother and the poor girl and I are tormented almost
to death. All this can be easily relieved. Believe me, it is possible
to live as cheaply in expensive Vienna as anywhere else; it all
depends on the housekeeping and the orderliness which is never

to be found in a young man, especially if he be in love. Whoever gets a wife such as I am going to have can count himself fortunate. We shall live simply and quietly, and yet be happy. Do not worry; for should I (which God forefend!) get ill to-day, especially if I were married, I wager that the first of the nobility would come to my help. . . . I await your consent with longing, best of fathers, I await it with confidence, my honor and fame depend upon it.

Vienna, July 27, 1782.

238. Meanwhile my striving is to secure a small certainty; then with the help of the contingencies, it will be easy to live here; and then to marry. I beg of you, dearest and best of fathers, listen to me! I have preferred my request, now listen to my reasons. The calls of nature are as strong in me, perhaps stronger, than in many a hulking fellow. I can not possibly live like the majority of our young men. In the first place I have too much religion, in the second too much love for my fellow man and too great a sense of honor ever to betray a girl. . . .

Vienna, December 15, 1781. [The whole of this letter deserves to be read by those who, misled by the reports, still deemed trustworthy when Jahn published the first edition of his great biography, believed that Mozart was a man of bad morals. Unfortunately Mozart's candor in presenting his case to his father can scarcely be adjusted to the requirements of a book designed for general circulation. Let it suffice that in his confession to his father Mozart puts himself on the ground of the loftiest sexual purity, and stakes life and death on the truthfulness of his statements. H. E. K.]

239. You surely can not be angry because I want to get married? I think and believe that you will recognize best my piety and honorable intentions in the circumstance. O, I could easily write a long answer to your last letter, and offer many objections; but my maxim is that it is not worth while to discuss matters that do not affect me. I can't help it,—it's my nature. I am really ashamed to defend myself when I find myself falsely accused; I always think, the truth will out some day.

Vienna, January 9, 1782, to his father. In the same letter he continues: "I can not be happy and contented without my dear Constanze, and without your satisfied acquiescence, I could only be half happy. Therefore, make me wholly happy."

240. As I have thought and said a thousand times, I would gladly leave everything in your hands with the greatest pleasure, but since, so to speak, it is useless to you but to my advantage, I deem it my duty to remember my wife and children.

June 16, 1787, to his sister, concerning his inheritance from his father, who had died on May 28.

241. Isn't it true that you are daily becoming more convinced of the truth of my corrective sermons? Is not the amusement of a fickle and capricious love far as the heavens from the blessedness which true, sensible love brings with it? Do you not often thank me in your heart for my instruction? You will soon make me vain! But joking aside, you do owe me a modicum of gratitude if you have made yourself worthy of Fräulein N., for I certainly did not play the smallest rôle at your conversion.

Prague, November 4, 1787, to a wealthy young friend, name unknown.

242. Pray believe anything you please about me but nothing ill. There are persons who believe it is impossible to love a poor girl without harboring wicked intentions; and the beautiful word mistress is so lovely!—I am a Mozart, but a young and well meaning Mozart. Among many faults I have this that I think that the friends who know me, know me. Hence many words are not necessary. If they do not know me where shall I find words enough? It is bad enough that words and letters are necessary.

Mannheim, February 22, 1778, to his father, who had rebuked him for falling in love with Aloysia Weber, who afterward became his sister-in-law.

RELIGION

Mozart was of a deeply religious nature, reared in Salzburg where his father was a member of the Archiepiscopal chapel. Throughout his life he remained a faithful son of the church, for whose servants, however, he had little sympathy. The one man whom Mozart hated from the bottom of his soul was Archbishop Hieronymus of Salzburg who sought to put all possible obstacles in the way of the youthful genius, and finally by the most infamous of acts covered himself everlastingly with infamy. Though Mozart frequently speaks angrily and bitterly of the priests, he always differentiates between religion, the church and their servants. Like Beethoven, Mozart stood toward God in the relationship of a child full of trust in his father. His reliance on Providence was so utter that his words sometimes sound almost fatalistic. His father harbored some rationalistic ideas which were even more pronounced in Mozart, so that he formed his own opinion concerning ecclesiastical ceremonies and occasionally disregarded them. His cheery temperament made it impossible that his religious life should be as profound as that of Beethoven.

243. I hope that with the help of God, Miss Martha will get well again. If not, you should not grieve too deeply, for God's will is always the best. God will know whether it is better to be in this world or the other.

Bologna, September 29, 1770, to his mother and sister in Salzburg. The young woman died soon after.

244. Tell papa to put aside his fears; I live with God ever before me. I recognize His omnipotence, I fear His anger; I ac-

knowledge His love, too, His compassion and mercy towards all His creatures; He will never desert those who serve Him. If matters go according to His will they go according to mine; consequently nothing can go wrong,—I must be satisfied and happy.

Augsburg, October 25, 1777, to his father, who was showering him with exhortations on the tour which he made with his mother through South Germany.

245. Let come what will, nothing can go ill so long as it is the will of God; and that it may so go is my daily prayer.

Mannheim, December 6, 1777, to his father. Mozart was waiting with some impatience to learn if he was to receive an appointment from Elector Karl Theodore. It did not come.

246. I know myself:—I know that I have so much religion that I shall never be able to do a thing which I would not be willing openly to do before the whole world; only the thought of meeting persons on my journeys whose ideas are radically different from mine (and those of all honest people) frightens me. Aside from that they may do what they please. I haven't the heart to travel with them, I would not have a single pleasant hour, I would not know what to say to them; in a word I do not trust them. Friends who have no religion are not stable.

Mannheim, February 2, 1778, to his father. For the reasons mentioned in the letter Mozart gave up his plan to travel to Paris with the musicians Wendling and Ramen. In truth, perhaps, his love affair with Aloysia Weber may have had something to do with his resolve.

247. I prayed to God for His mercy that all might go well, to His greater glory, and the symphony began. . . . Immediately after the symphony, full of joy, I went into the Palais Royal, ate an iced cream, prayed the rosary as I had promised to do, and went home. I am always best contented at home and always will be, or with a good, true, honest German.

Paris, July 3, 1778, to his father. The symphony in question is no longer in existence, although Mozart wanted to write it down again at a later date.

248. I must tell you my mother, my dear mother, is no more. —God has called her to Himself; He wanted her, I see that clearly, and I must submit to God's will. He gave her to me, and it was His to take her away. My friend, I am comforted, not but now, but long ago. By a singular grace of God I endured all with steadfastness and composure. When her illness grew dangerous I prayed God for two things only,—a happy hour of death for my mother, and strength and courage for myself. God heard me in His loving kindness, heard my prayer and bestowed the two mercies in largest measure.

Paris, July 3, 1778, to his good friend Bullinger, in Salzburg, who was commissioned gently to bear the intelligence to Mozart's father. At the same time Mozart, with considerate deception, wrote to his father about his mother's illness without mentioning her death.

249. I believe, and nothing shall ever persuade me differently, that no doctor, no man, no accident, can either give life to man or take it away; it rests with God alone. Those are only the instruments which He generally uses, though not always; we see men sink down and fall over dead. When the time is come no remedies can avail,—they accelerate death rather than retard it. . . . I do not say, therefore, that my mother will and must die, that all hope is gone; she may recover and again be well and sound,—but only if it is God's will.

Paris, July 3, 1778, to his father, from whom he is concealing the fact that his mother is dead. He is seeking to prepare him for the intelligence which he has already commissioned Bullinger to convey to the family.

250. Under those melancholy circumstances I comforted myself with three things, viz.: my complete and trustful submission to the will of God, then the realization of her easy and beautiful death, combined with the thought of the happiness which was to come to her in a moment,—how much happier she now is than we, so that we might even have wished to make the journey with her. Out of this wish and desire there was developed my third comfort, namely, that she is not lost to us forever, that we shall see her again, that we shall be together more joyous and

happy than ever we were in this world. It is only the time that is unknown, and that fact does not frighten me. When it is God's will, it shall be mine. Only the divine, the most sacred will be done; let us then pray a devout "Our Father" for her soul and proceed to other matters; everything has its time.

Paris, July 9, 1778, to his father, informing him of his mother's death.

251. Be without concern touching my soul's welfare, best of fathers! I am an erring young man, like so many others, but I can say to my own comfort, that I wish all were as little erring as I. You, perhaps, believe things about me which are not true. My chief fault is that I do not always appear to act as I ought. It is not true that I boasted that I eat fish every fast-day; but I did say that I was indifferent on the subject and did not consider it a sin, for in my case fasting means breaking off, eating less than usual. I hear mass every Sunday and holy day, and when it is possible on week days also,—you know that, my father.

Vienna, June 13, 1781—another attempt at justification against slander.

252. Moreover take the assurance that I certainly am religious, and if I should ever have the misfortune (which God will forefend) to go astray, I shall acquit you, best of fathers, from all blame. I alone would be the scoundrel; to you I owe all my spiritual and temporal welfare and salvation.

Vienna, June 13, 1781.

253. For a considerable time before we were married we went together to Holy Mass, to confession and to communion; and I found that I never prayed so fervently, confessed and communicated so devoutly, as when I was at her side;—and her experience was the same. In a word we were made for each other, and God, who ordains all things and consequently has ordained this, will not desert us. We both thank you obediently for your paternal blessing.

Vienna, August 17, 1782.

254. I have made it a habit in all things to imagine the worst. Inasmuch as, strictly speaking, death is the real aim of our life, I have for the past few years made myself acquainted with this true, best friend of mankind, so that the vision not only has no terror for me but much that is quieting and comforting. And I thank my God that He gave me the happiness and the opportunity (you understand me) to learn to know Him as the key to true blessedness.

Vienna, April 4, 1787, to his father, who died on the 28th of the following month. One of the few passages in Mozart's letters in which there are suggestions of the teachings of Freemasonry. In 1785 he had persuaded his father to join the order, with the result that new warmth was restored to the relationship which had cooled somewhat after Mozart's marriage.

255. To me that again is art twaddle! There may be something true in it for you enlightened Protestants, as you call yourselves, when you have your religion in your heads; I can not tell. But you do not feel what *Agnus Dei, qui tollis peccata mundi* and such things mean. But when one, like I, has been initiated from earliest childhood in the mystical sanctuary of our religion; when there one does not know whither to go with all the vague but urgent feelings, but waits with a heart full of devotion for the divine service without really knowing what to expect, yet rises lightened and uplifted without knowing what one has received; when one deemed those fortunate who knelt under the touching strains of the *Agnus Dei* and received the sacrament, and at the moment of reception the music spoke in gentle joy from the hearts of the kneeling ones, *Benedictus qui venit, etc.;* —then it is a different matter. True, it is lost in the hurly-burly of life; but,—at least it is so in my case,—when you take up the words which you have heard a thousand times, for the purpose of setting them to music, everything comes back and you feel your soul moved again.

Spoken in Leipsic, in 1789, when somebody expressed pity for those capable musicians who were obliged to "employ their powers on ecclesiastical subjects, which were mostly not only unfruitful but intellectually killing." Rochlitz reports the utterance but does not vouch for its literalness.

A CATALOG OF SELECTED
DOVER BOOKS
IN ALL FIELDS OF INTEREST

A CATALOG OF SELECTED DOVER
BOOKS IN ALL FIELDS OF INTEREST

DRAWINGS OF REMBRANDT, edited by Seymour Slive. Updated Lippmann, Hofstede de Groot edition, with definitive scholarly apparatus. All portraits, biblical sketches, landscapes, nudes. Oriental figures, classical studies, together with selection of work by followers. 550 illustrations. Total of 630pp. 9⅛ × 12¼.
21485-0, 21486-9 Pa., Two-vol. set $25.00

GHOST AND HORROR STORIES OF AMBROSE BIERCE, Ambrose Bierce. 24 tales vividly imagined, strangely prophetic, and decades ahead of their time in technical skill: "The Damned Thing," "An Inhabitant of Carcosa," "The Eyes of the Panther," "Moxon's Master," and 20 more. 199pp. 5⅜ × 8½. 20767-6 Pa. $3.95

ETHICAL WRITINGS OF MAIMONIDES, Maimonides. Most significant ethical works of great medieval sage, newly translated for utmost precision, readability. Laws Concerning Character Traits, Eight Chapters, more. 192pp. 5⅜ × 8½.
24522-5 Pa. $4.50

THE EXPLORATION OF THE COLORADO RIVER AND ITS CANYONS, J. W. Powell. Full text of Powell's 1,000-mile expedition down the fabled Colorado in 1869. Superb account of terrain, geology, vegetation, Indians, famine, mutiny, treacherous rapids, mighty canyons, during exploration of last unknown part of continental U.S. 400pp. 5⅜ × 8½. 20094-9 Pa. $6.95

HISTORY OF PHILOSOPHY, Julián Marías. Clearest one-volume history on the market. Every major philosopher and dozens of others, to Existentialism and later. 505pp. 5⅜ × 8½. 21739-6 Pa. $8.50

ALL ABOUT LIGHTNING, Martin A. Uman. Highly readable non-technical survey of nature and causes of lightning, thunderstorms, ball lightning, St. Elmo's Fire, much more. Illustrated. 192pp. 5⅜ × 8½. 25237-X Pa. $5.95

SAILING ALONE AROUND THE WORLD, Captain Joshua Slocum. First man to sail around the world, alone, in small boat. One of great feats of seamanship told in delightful manner. 67 illustrations. 294pp. 5⅜ × 8½. 20326-3 Pa. $4.95

LETTERS AND NOTES ON THE MANNERS, CUSTOMS AND CONDITIONS OF THE NORTH AMERICAN INDIANS, George Catlin. Classic account of life among Plains Indians: ceremonies, hunt, warfare, etc. 312 plates. 572pp. of text. 6⅛ × 9¼. 22118-0, 22119-9 Pa. Two-vol. set $15.90

ALASKA: The Harriman Expedition, 1899, John Burroughs, John Muir, et al. Informative, engrossing accounts of two-month, 9,000-mile expedition. Native peoples, wildlife, forests, geography, salmon industry, glaciers, more. Profusely illustrated. 240 black-and-white line drawings. 124 black-and-white photographs. 3 maps. Index. 576pp. 5⅜ × 8½. 25109-8 Pa. $11.95

THE BOOK OF BEASTS: Being a Translation from a Latin Bestiary of the Twelfth Century, T. H. White. Wonderful catalog real and fanciful beasts: manticore, griffin, phoenix, amphivius, jaculus, many more. White's witty erudite commentary on scientific, historical aspects. Fascinating glimpse of medieval mind. Illustrated. 296pp. 5⅜ × 8¼. (Available in U.S. only) 24609-4 Pa. $5.95

FRANK LLOYD WRIGHT: ARCHITECTURE AND NATURE With 160 Illustrations, Donald Hoffmann. Profusely illustrated study of influence of nature—especially prairie—on Wright's designs for Fallingwater, Robie House, Guggenheim Museum, other masterpieces. 96pp. 9¼ × 10¾. 25098-9 Pa. $7.95

FRANK LLOYD WRIGHT'S FALLINGWATER, Donald Hoffmann. Wright's famous waterfall house: planning and construction of organic idea. History of site, owners, Wright's personal involvement. Photographs of various stages of building. Preface by Edgar Kaufmann, Jr. 100 illustrations. 112pp. 9¼ × 10.
23671-4 Pa. $7.95

YEARS WITH FRANK LLOYD WRIGHT: Apprentice to Genius, Edgar Tafel. Insightful memoir by a former apprentice presents a revealing portrait of Wright the man, the inspired teacher, the greatest American architect. 372 black-and-white illustrations. Preface. Index. vi + 228pp. 8¼ × 11. 24801-1 Pa. $9.95

THE STORY OF KING ARTHUR AND HIS KNIGHTS, Howard Pyle. Enchanting version of King Arthur fable has delighted generations with imaginative narratives of exciting adventures and unforgettable illustrations by the author. 41 illustrations. xviii + 313pp. 6⅛ × 9¼. 21445-1 Pa. $5.95

THE GODS OF THE EGYPTIANS, E. A. Wallis Budge. Thorough coverage of numerous gods of ancient Egypt by foremost Egyptologist. Information on evolution of cults, rites and gods; the cult of Osiris; the Book of the Dead and its rites; the sacred animals and birds; Heaven and Hell; and more. 956pp. 6⅛ × 9¼.
22055-9, 22056-7 Pa., Two-vol. set $21.90

A THEOLOGICO-POLITICAL TREATISE, Benedict Spinoza. Also contains unfinished *Political Treatise*. Great classic on religious liberty, theory of government on common consent. R. Elwes translation. Total of 421pp. 5⅜ × 8½.
20249-6 Pa. $6.95

INCIDENTS OF TRAVEL IN CENTRAL AMERICA, CHIAPAS, AND YUCATAN, John L. Stephens. Almost single-handed discovery of Maya culture; exploration of ruined cities, monuments, temples; customs of Indians. 115 drawings. 892pp. 5⅜ × 8½. 22404-X, 22405-8 Pa., Two-vol. set $15.90

LOS CAPRICHOS, Francisco Goya. 80 plates of wild, grotesque monsters and caricatures. Prado manuscript included. 183pp. 6⅝ × 9⅝. 22384-1 Pa. $4.95

AUTOBIOGRAPHY: The Story of My Experiments with Truth, Mohandas K. Gandhi. Not hagiography, but Gandhi in his own words. Boyhood, legal studies, purification, the growth of the Satyagraha (nonviolent protest) movement. Critical, inspiring work of the man who freed India. 480pp. 5⅜ × 8½. (Available in U.S. only)
24593-4 Pa. $6.95

ILLUSTRATED DICTIONARY OF HISTORIC ARCHITECTURE, edited by Cyril M. Harris. Extraordinary compendium of clear, concise definitions for over 5,000 important architectural terms complemented by over 2,000 line drawings. Covers full spectrum of architecture from ancient ruins to 20th-century Modernism. Preface. 592pp. 7½ × 9⅝. 24444-X Pa. $14.95

THE NIGHT BEFORE CHRISTMAS, Clement Moore. Full text, and woodcuts from original 1848 book. Also critical, historical material. 19 illustrations. 40pp. 4⅝ × 6. 22797-9 Pa. $2.50

THE LESSON OF JAPANESE ARCHITECTURE: 165 Photographs, Jiro Harada. Memorable gallery of 165 photographs taken in the 1930's of exquisite Japanese homes of the well-to-do and historic buildings. 13 line diagrams. 192pp. 8⅜ × 11¼. 24778-3 Pa. $8.95

THE AUTOBIOGRAPHY OF CHARLES DARWIN AND SELECTED LETTERS, edited by Francis Darwin. The fascinating life of eccentric genius composed of an intimate memoir by Darwin (intended for his children); commentary by his son, Francis; hundreds of fragments from notebooks, journals, papers; and letters to and from Lyell, Hooker, Huxley, Wallace and Henslow. xi + 365pp. 5⅜ × 8. 20479-0 Pa. $5.95

WONDERS OF THE SKY: Observing Rainbows, Comets, Eclipses, the Stars and Other Phenomena, Fred Schaaf. Charming, easy-to-read poetic guide to all manner of celestial events visible to the naked eye. Mock suns, glories, Belt of Venus, more. Illustrated. 299pp. 5¼ × 8¼. 24402-4 Pa. $7.95

BURNHAM'S CELESTIAL HANDBOOK, Robert Burnham, Jr. Thorough guide to the stars beyond our solar system. Exhaustive treatment. Alphabetical by constellation: Andromeda to Cetus in Vol. 1; Chamaeleon to Orion in Vol. 2; and Pavo to Vulpecula in Vol. 3. Hundreds of illustrations. Index in Vol. 3. 2,000pp. 6⅛ × 9¼. 23567-X, 23568-8, 23673-0 Pa., Three-vol. set $37.85

STAR NAMES: Their Lore and Meaning, Richard Hinckley Allen. Fascinating history of names various cultures have given to constellations and literary and folkloristic uses that have been made of stars. Indexes to subjects. Arabic and Greek names. Biblical references. Bibliography. 563pp. 5⅜ × 8½. 21079-0 Pa. $7.95

THIRTY YEARS THAT SHOOK PHYSICS: The Story of Quantum Theory, George Gamow. Lucid, accessible introduction to influential theory of energy and matter. Careful explanations of Dirac's anti-particles, Bohr's model of the atom, much more. 12 plates. Numerous drawings. 240pp. 5⅜ × 8½. 24895-X Pa. $4.95

CHINESE DOMESTIC FURNITURE IN PHOTOGRAPHS AND MEASURED DRAWINGS, Gustav Ecke. A rare volume, now affordably priced for antique collectors, furniture buffs and art historians. Detailed review of styles ranging from early Shang to late Ming. Unabridged republication. 161 black-and-white drawings, photos. Total of 224pp. 8⅜ × 11¼. (Available in U.S. only) 25171-3 Pa. $12.95

VINCENT VAN GOGH: A Biography, Julius Meier-Graefe. Dynamic, penetrating study of artist's life, relationship with brother, Theo, painting techniques, travels, more. Readable, engrossing. 160pp. 5⅜ × 8½. (Available in U.S. only) 25253-1 Pa. $3.95

HOW TO WRITE, Gertrude Stein. Gertrude Stein claimed anyone could understand her unconventional writing—here are clues to help. Fascinating improvisations, language experiments, explanations illuminate Stein's craft and the art of writing. Total of 414pp. 4⅝ × 6⅜. 23144-5 Pa. $5.95

ADVENTURES AT SEA IN THE GREAT AGE OF SAIL: Five Firsthand Narratives, edited by Elliot Snow. Rare true accounts of exploration, whaling, shipwreck, fierce natives, trade, shipboard life, more. 33 illustrations. Introduction. 353pp. 5⅜ × 8½. 25177-2 Pa. $7.95

THE HERBAL OR GENERAL HISTORY OF PLANTS, John Gerard. Classic descriptions of about 2,850 plants—with over 2,700 illustrations—includes Latin and English names, physical descriptions, varieties, time and place of growth, more. 2,706 illustrations. xlv + 1,678pp. 8½ × 12¼. 23147-X Cloth. $75.00

DOROTHY AND THE WIZARD IN OZ, L. Frank Baum. Dorothy and the Wizard visit the center of the Earth, where people are vegetables, glass houses grow and Oz characters reappear. Classic sequel to Wizard of Oz. 256pp. 5⅜ × 8. 24714-7 Pa. $4.95

SONGS OF EXPERIENCE: Facsimile Reproduction with 26 Plates in Full Color, William Blake. This facsimile of Blake's original "Illuminated Book" reproduces 26 full-color plates from a rare 1826 edition. Includes "The Tyger," "London," "Holy Thursday," and other immortal poems. 26 color plates. Printed text of poems. 48pp. 5¼ × 7. 24636-1 Pa. $3.50

SONGS OF INNOCENCE, William Blake. The first and most popular of Blake's famous "Illuminated Books," in a facsimile edition reproducing all 31 brightly colored plates. Additional printed text of each poem. 64pp. 5¼ × 7. 22764-2 Pa. $3.50

PRECIOUS STONES, Max Bauer. Classic, thorough study of diamonds, rubies, emeralds, garnets, etc.: physical character, occurrence, properties, use, similar topics. 20 plates, 8 in color. 94 figures. 659pp. 6⅛ × 9¼. 21910-0, 21911-9 Pa., Two-vol. set $15.90

ENCYCLOPEDIA OF VICTORIAN NEEDLEWORK, S. F. A. Caulfeild and Blanche Saward. Full, precise descriptions of stitches, techniques for dozens of needlecrafts—most exhaustive reference of its kind. Over 800 figures. Total of 679pp. 8⅜ × 11. Two volumes. Vol. 1 22800-2 Pa. $11.95
Vol. 2 22801-0 Pa. $11.95

THE MARVELOUS LAND OF OZ, L. Frank Baum. Second Oz book, the Scarecrow and Tin Woodman are back with hero named Tip, Oz magic. 136 illustrations. 287pp. 5⅜ × 8½. 20692-0 Pa. $5.95

WILD FOWL DECOYS, Joel Barber. Basic book on the subject, by foremost authority and collector. Reveals history of decoy making and rigging, place in American culture, different kinds of decoys, how to make them, and how to use them. 140 plates. 156pp. 7⅞ × 10¾. 20011-6 Pa. $8.95

HISTORY OF LACE, Mrs. Bury Palliser. Definitive, profusely illustrated chronicle of lace from earliest times to late 19th century. Laces of Italy, Greece, England, France, Belgium, etc. Landmark of needlework scholarship. 266 illustrations. 672pp. 6⅛ × 9¼. 24742-2 Pa. $14.95

ILLUSTRATED GUIDE TO SHAKER FURNITURE, Robert Meader. All furniture and appurtenances, with much on unknown local styles. 235 photos. 146pp. 9 × 12. 22819-3 Pa. $7.95

WHALE SHIPS AND WHALING: A Pictorial Survey, George Francis Dow. Over 200 vintage engravings, drawings, photographs of barks, brigs, cutters, other vessels. Also harpoons, lances, whaling guns, many other artifacts. Comprehensive text by foremost authority. 207 black-and-white illustrations. 288pp. 6 × 9. 24808-9 Pa. $8.95

THE BERTRAMS, Anthony Trollope. Powerful portrayal of blind self-will and thwarted ambition includes one of Trollope's most heartrending love stories. 497pp. 5⅜ × 8½. 25119-5 Pa. $8.95

ADVENTURES WITH A HAND LENS, Richard Headstrom. Clearly written guide to observing and studying flowers and grasses, fish scales, moth and insect wings, egg cases, buds, feathers, seeds, leaf scars, moss, molds, ferns, common crystals, etc.—all with an ordinary, inexpensive magnifying glass. 209 exact line drawings aid in your discoveries. 220pp. 5⅜ × 8½. 23330-8 Pa. $4.50

RODIN ON ART AND ARTISTS, Auguste Rodin. Great sculptor's candid, wide-ranging comments on meaning of art; great artists; relation of sculpture to poetry, painting, music; philosophy of life, more. 76 superb black-and-white illustrations of Rodin's sculpture, drawings and prints. 119pp. 8⅜ × 11¼. 24487-3 Pa. $6.95

FIFTY CLASSIC FRENCH FILMS, 1912–1982: A Pictorial Record, Anthony Slide. Memorable stills from Grand Illusion, Beauty and the Beast, Hiroshima, Mon Amour, many more. Credits, plot synopses, reviews, etc. 160pp. 8¼ × 11. 25256-6 Pa. $11.95

THE PRINCIPLES OF PSYCHOLOGY, William James. Famous long course complete, unabridged. Stream of thought, time perception, memory, experimental methods; great work decades ahead of its time. 94 figures. 1,391pp. 5⅜ × 8½. 20381-6, 20382-4 Pa., Two-vol. set $19.90

BODIES IN A BOOKSHOP, R. T. Campbell. Challenging mystery of blackmail and murder with ingenious plot and superbly drawn characters. In the best tradition of British suspense fiction. 192pp. 5⅜ × 8½. 24720-1 Pa. $3.95

CALLAS: PORTRAIT OF A PRIMA DONNA, George Jellinek. Renowned commentator on the musical scene chronicles incredible career and life of the most controversial, fascinating, influential operatic personality of our time. 64 black-and-white photographs. 416pp. 5⅜ × 8¼. 25047-4 Pa. $7.95

GEOMETRY, RELATIVITY AND THE FOURTH DIMENSION, Rudolph Rucker. Exposition of fourth dimension, concepts of relativity as Flatland characters continue adventures. Popular, easily followed yet accurate, profound. 141 illustrations. 133pp. 5⅜ × 8½. 23400-2 Pa. $3.50

HOUSEHOLD STORIES BY THE BROTHERS GRIMM, with pictures by Walter Crane. 53 classic stories—Rumpelstiltskin, Rapunzel, Hansel and Gretel, the Fisherman and his Wife, Snow White, Tom Thumb, Sleeping Beauty, Cinderella, and so much more—lavishly illustrated with original 19th century drawings. 114 illustrations. x + 269pp. 5⅜ × 8½. 21080-4 Pa. $4.50

CATALOG OF DOVER BOOKS

SUNDIALS, Albert Waugh. Far and away the best, most thorough coverage of ideas, mathematics concerned, types, construction, adjusting anywhere. Over 100 illustrations. 230pp. 5⅜ × 8½. 22947-5 Pa. $4.50

PICTURE HISTORY OF THE NORMANDIE: With 190 Illustrations, Frank O. Braynard. Full story of legendary French ocean liner: Art Deco interiors, design innovations, furnishings, celebrities, maiden voyage, tragic fire, much more. Extensive text. 144pp. 8⅜ × 11¼. 25257-4 Pa. $9.95

THE FIRST AMERICAN COOKBOOK: A Facsimile of "American Cookery," 1796, Amelia Simmons. Facsimile of the first American-written cookbook published in the United States contains authentic recipes for colonial favorites— pumpkin pudding, winter squash pudding, spruce beer, Indian slapjacks, and more. Introductory Essay and Glossary of colonial cooking terms. 80pp. 5⅜ × 8½. 24710-4 Pa. $3.50

101 PUZZLES IN THOUGHT AND LOGIC, C. R. Wylie, Jr. Solve murders and robberies, find out which fishermen are liars, how a blind man could possibly identify a color—purely by your own reasoning! 107pp. 5⅜ × 8½. 20367-0 Pa. $2.50

THE BOOK OF WORLD-FAMOUS MUSIC—CLASSICAL, POPULAR AND FOLK, James J. Fuld. Revised and enlarged republication of landmark work in musico-bibliography. Full information about nearly 1,000 songs and compositions including first lines of music and lyrics. New supplement. Index. 800pp. 5⅜ × 8¼. 24857-7 Pa. $14.95

ANTHROPOLOGY AND MODERN LIFE, Franz Boas. Great anthropologist's classic treatise on race and culture. Introduction by Ruth Bunzel. Only inexpensive paperback edition. 255pp. 5⅜ × 8½. 25245-0 Pa. $5.95

THE TALE OF PETER RABBIT, Beatrix Potter. The inimitable Peter's terrifying adventure in Mr. McGregor's garden, with all 27 wonderful, full-color Potter illustrations. 55pp. 4¼ × 5½. (Available in U.S. only) 22827-4 Pa. $1.75

THREE PROPHETIC SCIENCE FICTION NOVELS, H. G. Wells. *When the Sleeper Wakes, A Story of the Days to Come* and *The Time Machine* (full version). 335pp. 5⅜ × 8½. (Available in U.S. only) 20605-X Pa. $5.95

APICIUS COOKERY AND DINING IN IMPERIAL ROME, edited and translated by Joseph Dommers Vehling. Oldest known cookbook in existence offers readers a clear picture of what foods Romans ate, how they prepared them, etc. 49 illustrations. 301pp. 6½ × 9¼. 23563-7 Pa. $6.50

SHAKESPEARE LEXICON AND QUOTATION DICTIONARY, Alexander Schmidt. Full definitions, locations, shades of meaning of every word in plays and poems. More than 50,000 exact quotations. 1,485pp. 6½ × 9¼. 22726-X, 22727-8 Pa., Two-vol. set $27.90

THE WORLD'S GREAT SPEECHES, edited by Lewis Copeland and Lawrence W. Lamm. Vast collection of 278 speeches from Greeks to 1970. Powerful and effective models; unique look at history. 842pp. 5⅜ × 8½. 20468-5 Pa. $11.95

THE BLUE FAIRY BOOK, Andrew Lang. The first, most famous collection, with many familiar tales: Little Red Riding Hood, Aladdin and the Wonderful Lamp, Puss in Boots, Sleeping Beauty, Hansel and Gretel, Rumpelstiltskin; 37 in all. 138 illustrations. 390pp. 5⅜ × 8½.   21437-0 Pa. $5.95

THE STORY OF THE CHAMPIONS OF THE ROUND TABLE, Howard Pyle. Sir Launcelot, Sir Tristram and Sir Percival in spirited adventures of love and triumph retold in Pyle's inimitable style. 50 drawings, 31 full-page. xviii + 329pp. 6½ × 9¼.   21883-X Pa. $6.95

AUDUBON AND HIS JOURNALS, Maria Audubon. Unmatched two-volume portrait of the great artist, naturalist and author contains his journals, an excellent biography by his granddaughter, expert annotations by the noted ornithologist, Dr. Elliott Coues, and 37 superb illustrations. Total of 1,200pp. 5⅜ × 8.
Vol. I 25143-8 Pa. $8.95
Vol. II 25144-6 Pa. $8.95

GREAT DINOSAUR HUNTERS AND THEIR DISCOVERIES, Edwin H. Colbert. Fascinating, lavishly illustrated chronicle of dinosaur research, 1820's to 1960. Achievements of Cope, Marsh, Brown, Buckland, Mantell, Huxley, many others. 384pp. 5¼ × 8¼.   24701-5 Pa. $6.95

THE TASTEMAKERS, Russell Lynes. Informal, illustrated social history of American taste 1850's–1950's. First popularized categories Highbrow, Lowbrow, Middlebrow. 129 illustrations. New (1979) afterword. 384pp. 6 × 9.
23993-4 Pa. $6.95

DOUBLE CROSS PURPOSES, Ronald A. Knox. A treasure hunt in the Scottish Highlands, an old map, unidentified corpse, surprise discoveries keep reader guessing in this cleverly intricate tale of financial skullduggery. 2 black-and-white maps. 320pp. 5⅜ × 8½. (Available in U.S. only)   25032-6 Pa. $5.95

AUTHENTIC VICTORIAN DECORATION AND ORNAMENTATION IN FULL COLOR: 46 Plates from "Studies in Design," Christopher Dresser. Superb full-color lithographs reproduced from rare original portfolio of a major Victorian designer. 48pp. 9¼ × 12¼.   25083-0 Pa. $7.95

PRIMITIVE ART, Franz Boas. Remains the best text ever prepared on subject, thoroughly discussing Indian, African, Asian, Australian, and, especially, Northern American primitive art. Over 950 illustrations show ceramics, masks, totem poles, weapons, textiles, paintings, much more. 376pp. 5⅜ × 8.   20025-6 Pa. $6.95

SIDELIGHTS ON RELATIVITY, Albert Einstein. Unabridged republication of two lectures delivered by the great physicist in 1920–21. *Ether and Relativity* and *Geometry and Experience*. Elegant ideas in non-mathematical form, accessible to intelligent layman. vi + 56pp. 5⅜ × 8½.   24511-X Pa. $2.95

THE WIT AND HUMOR OF OSCAR WILDE, edited by Alvin Redman. More than 1,000 ripostes, paradoxes, wisecracks: Work is the curse of the drinking classes, I can resist everything except temptation, etc. 258pp. 5⅜ × 8½.   20602-5 Pa. $4.50

ADVENTURES WITH A MICROSCOPE, Richard Headstrom. 59 adventures with clothing fibers, protozoa, ferns and lichens, roots and leaves, much more. 142 illustrations. 232pp. 5⅜ × 8½.   23471-1 Pa. $3.95

PLANTS OF THE BIBLE, Harold N. Moldenke and Alma L. Moldenke. Standard reference to all 230 plants mentioned in Scriptures. Latin name, biblical reference, uses, modern identity, much more. Unsurpassed encyclopedic resource for scholars, botanists, nature lovers, students of Bible. Bibliography. Indexes. 123 black-and-white illustrations. 384pp. 6 × 9. 25069-5 Pa. $8.95

FAMOUS AMERICAN WOMEN: A Biographical Dictionary from Colonial Times to the Present, Robert McHenry, ed. From Pocahontas to Rosa Parks, 1,035 distinguished American women documented in separate biographical entries. Accurate, up-to-date data, numerous categories, spans 400 years. Indices. 493pp. 6½ × 9¼. 24523-3 Pa. $9.95

THE FABULOUS INTERIORS OF THE GREAT OCEAN LINERS IN HISTORIC PHOTOGRAPHS, William H. Miller, Jr. Some 200 superb photographs capture exquisite interiors of world's great "floating palaces"—1890's to 1980's: *Titanic, Ile de France, Queen Elizabeth, United States, Europa,* more. Approx. 200 black-and-white photographs. Captions. Text. Introduction. 160pp. 8⅞ × 11¾. 24756-2 Pa. $9.95

THE GREAT LUXURY LINERS, 1927-1954: A Photographic Record, William H. Miller, Jr. Nostalgic tribute to heyday of ocean liners. 186 photos of Ile de France, Normandie, Leviathan, Queen Elizabeth, United States, many others. Interior and exterior views. Introduction. Captions. 160pp. 9 × 12. 24056-8 Pa. $9.95

A NATURAL HISTORY OF THE DUCKS, John Charles Phillips. Great landmark of ornithology offers complete detailed coverage of nearly 200 species and subspecies of ducks: gadwall, sheldrake, merganser, pintail, many more. 74 full-color plates, 102 black-and-white. Bibliography. Total of 1,920pp. 8⅝ × 11¼. 25141-1, 25142-X Cloth. Two-vol. set $100.00

THE SEAWEED HANDBOOK: An Illustrated Guide to Seaweeds from North Carolina to Canada, Thomas F. Lee. Concise reference covers 78 species. Scientific and common names, habitat, distribution, more. Finding keys for easy identification. 224pp. 5⅜ × 8½. 25215-9 Pa. $5.95

THE TEN BOOKS OF ARCHITECTURE: The 1755 Leoni Edition, Leon Battista Alberti. Rare classic helped introduce the glories of ancient architecture to the Renaissance. 68 black-and-white plates. 336pp. 8⅜ × 11¼. 25239-6 Pa. $14.95

MISS MACKENZIE, Anthony Trollope. Minor masterpieces by Victorian master unmasks many truths about life in 19th-century England. First inexpensive edition in years. 392pp. 5⅜ × 8½. 25201-9 Pa. $7.95

THE RIME OF THE ANCIENT MARINER, Gustave Doré, Samuel Taylor Coleridge. Dramatic engravings considered by many to be his greatest work. The terrifying space of the open sea, the storms and whirlpools of an unknown ocean, the ice of Antarctica, more—all rendered in a powerful, chilling manner. Full text. 38 plates. 77pp. 9¼ × 12. 22305-1 Pa. $4.95

THE EXPEDITIONS OF ZEBULON MONTGOMERY PIKE, Zebulon Montgomery Pike. Fascinating first-hand accounts (1805-6) of exploration of Mississippi River, Indian wars, capture by Spanish dragoons, much more. 1,088pp. 5⅜ × 8½. 25254-X, 25255-8 Pa. Two-vol. set $23.90

A CONCISE HISTORY OF PHOTOGRAPHY: Third Revised Edition, Helmut Gernsheim. Best one-volume history—camera obscura, photochemistry, daguerreotypes, evolution of cameras, film, more. Also artistic aspects—landscape, portraits, fine art, etc. 281 black-and-white photographs. 26 in color. 176pp. 8⅜ × 11¼. 25128-4 Pa. $12.95

THE DORÉ BIBLE ILLUSTRATIONS, Gustave Doré. 241 detailed plates from the Bible: the Creation scenes, Adam and Eve, Flood, Babylon, battle sequences, life of Jesus, etc. Each plate is accompanied by the verses from the King James version of the Bible. 241pp. 9 × 12. 23004-X Pa. $8.95

HUGGER-MUGGER IN THE LOUVRE, Elliot Paul. Second Homer Evans mystery-comedy. Theft at the Louvre involves sleuth in hilarious, madcap caper. "A knockout."—Books. 336pp. 5⅜ × 8½. 25185-3 Pa. $5.95

FLATLAND, E. A. Abbott. Intriguing and enormously popular science-fiction classic explores the complexities of trying to survive as a two-dimensional being in a three-dimensional world. Amusingly illustrated by the author. 16 illustrations. 103pp. 5⅜ × 8½. 20001-9 Pa. $2.25

THE HISTORY OF THE LEWIS AND CLARK EXPEDITION, Meriwether Lewis and William Clark, edited by Elliott Coues. Classic edition of Lewis and Clark's day-by-day journals that later became the basis for U.S. claims to Oregon and the West. Accurate and invaluable geographical, botanical, biological, meteorological and anthropological material. Total of 1,508pp. 5⅜ × 8½.
21268-8, 21269-6, 21270-X Pa. Three-vol. set $25.50

LANGUAGE, TRUTH AND LOGIC, Alfred J. Ayer. Famous, clear introduction to Vienna, Cambridge schools of Logical Positivism. Role of philosophy, elimination of metaphysics, nature of analysis, etc. 160pp. 5⅜ × 8½. (Available in U.S. and Canada only) 20010-8 Pa. $2.95

MATHEMATICS FOR THE NONMATHEMATICIAN, Morris Kline. Detailed, college-level treatment of mathematics in cultural and historical context, with numerous exercises. For liberal arts students. Preface. Recommended Reading Lists. Tables. Index. Numerous black-and-white figures. xvi + 641pp. 5⅜ × 8½.
24823-2 Pa. $11.95

28 SCIENCE FICTION STORIES, H. G. Wells. Novels, *Star Begotten* and *Men Like Gods,* plus 26 short stories: "Empire of the Ants," "A Story of the Stone Age," "The Stolen Bacillus," "In the Abyss," etc. 915pp. 5⅜ × 8½. (Available in U.S. only)
20265-8 Cloth. $10.95

HANDBOOK OF PICTORIAL SYMBOLS, Rudolph Modley. 3,250 signs and symbols, many systems in full; official or heavy commercial use. Arranged by subject. Most in Pictorial Archive series. 143pp. 8⅛ × 11. 23357-X Pa. $5.95

INCIDENTS OF TRAVEL IN YUCATAN, John L. Stephens. Classic (1843) exploration of jungles of Yucatan, looking for evidences of Maya civilization. Travel adventures, Mexican and Indian culture, etc. Total of 669pp. 5⅜ × 8½.
20926-1, 20927-X Pa., Two-vol. set $9.90

DEGAS: An Intimate Portrait, Ambroise Vollard. Charming, anecdotal memoir by famous art dealer of one of the greatest 19th-century French painters. 14 black-and-white illustrations. Introduction by Harold L. Van Doren. 96pp. 5⅜ × 8½.
25131-4 Pa. $3.95

PERSONAL NARRATIVE OF A PILGRIMAGE TO ALMANDINAH AND MECCAH, Richard Burton. Great travel classic by remarkably colorful personality. Burton, disguised as a Moroccan, visited sacred shrines of Islam, narrowly escaping death. 47 illustrations. 959pp. 5⅜ × 8½. 21217-3, 21218-1 Pa., Two-vol. set $17.90

PHRASE AND WORD ORIGINS, A. H. Holt. Entertaining, reliable, modern study of more than 1,200 colorful words, phrases, origins and histories. Much unexpected information. 254pp. 5⅜ × 8½. 20758-7 Pa. $5.95

THE RED THUMB MARK, R. Austin Freeman. In this first Dr. Thorndyke case, the great scientific detective draws fascinating conclusions from the nature of a single fingerprint. Exciting story, authentic science. 320pp. 5⅜ × 8½. (Available in U.S. only) 25210-8 Pa. $5.95

AN EGYPTIAN HIEROGLYPHIC DICTIONARY, E. A. Wallis Budge. Monumental work containing about 25,000 words or terms that occur in texts ranging from 3000 B.C. to 600 A.D. Each entry consists of a transliteration of the word, the word in hieroglyphs, and the meaning in English. 1,314pp. 6⅜ × 10.
23615-3, 23616-1 Pa., Two-vol. set $27.90

THE COMPLEAT STRATEGYST: Being a Primer on the Theory of Games of Strategy, J. D. Williams. Highly entertaining classic describes, with many illustrated examples, how to select best strategies in conflict situations. Prefaces. Appendices. xvi + 268pp. 5⅜ × 8½. 25101-2 Pa. $5.95

THE ROAD TO OZ, L. Frank Baum. Dorothy meets the Shaggy Man, little Button-Bright and the Rainbow's beautiful daughter in this delightful trip to the magical Land of Oz. 272pp. 5⅜ × 8. 25208-6 Pa. $4.95

POINT AND LINE TO PLANE, Wassily Kandinsky. Seminal exposition of role of point, line, other elements in non-objective painting. Essential to understanding 20th-century art. 127 illustrations. 192pp. 6½ × 9¼. 23808-3 Pa. $4.50

LADY ANNA, Anthony Trollope. Moving chronicle of Countess Lovel's bitter struggle to win for herself and daughter Anna their rightful rank and fortune—perhaps at cost of sanity itself. 384pp. 5⅜ × 8½. 24669-8 Pa. $6.95

EGYPTIAN MAGIC, E. A. Wallis Budge. Sums up all that is known about magic in Ancient Egypt: the role of magic in controlling the gods, powerful amulets that warded off evil spirits, scarabs of immortality, use of wax images, formulas and spells, the secret name, much more. 253pp. 5⅜ × 8½. 22681-6 Pa. $4.50

THE DANCE OF SIVA, Ananda Coomaraswamy. Preeminent authority unfolds the vast metaphysic of India: the revelation of her art, conception of the universe, social organization, etc. 27 reproductions of art masterpieces. 192pp. 5⅜ × 8½.
24817-8 Pa. $5.95

CHRISTMAS CUSTOMS AND TRADITIONS, Clement A. Miles. Origin, evolution, significance of religious, secular practices. Caroling, gifts, yule logs, much more. Full, scholarly yet fascinating; non-sectarian. 400pp. 5⅜ × 8½.
23354-5 Pa. $6.50

THE HUMAN FIGURE IN MOTION, Eadweard Muybridge. More than 4,500 stopped-action photos, in action series, showing undraped men, women, children jumping, lying down, throwing, sitting, wrestling, carrying, etc. 390pp. 7⅞ × 10⅝.
20204-6 Cloth. $19.95

THE MAN WHO WAS THURSDAY, Gilbert Keith Chesterton. Witty, fast-paced novel about a club of anarchists in turn-of-the-century London. Brilliant social, religious, philosophical speculations. 128pp. 5⅜ × 8½. 25121-7 Pa. $3.95

A CEZANNE SKETCHBOOK: Figures, Portraits, Landscapes and Still Lifes, Paul Cezanne. Great artist experiments with tonal effects, light, mass, other qualities in over 100 drawings. A revealing view of developing master painter, precursor of Cubism. 102 black-and-white illustrations. 144pp. 8¾ × 6⅜. 24790-2 Pa. $5.95

AN ENCYCLOPEDIA OF BATTLES: Accounts of Over 1,560 Battles from 1479 B.C. to the Present, David Eggenberger. Presents essential details of every major battle in recorded history, from the first battle of Megiddo in 1479 B.C. to Grenada in 1984. List of Battle Maps. New Appendix covering the years 1967–1984. Index. 99 illustrations. 544pp. 6½ × 9¼. 24913-1 Pa. $14.95

AN ETYMOLOGICAL DICTIONARY OF MODERN ENGLISH, Ernest Weekley. Richest, fullest work, by foremost British lexicographer. Detailed word histories. Inexhaustible. Total of 856pp. 6½ × 9¼.
21873-2, 21874-0 Pa., Two-vol. set $17.00

WEBSTER'S AMERICAN MILITARY BIOGRAPHIES, edited by Robert McHenry. Over 1,000 figures who shaped 3 centuries of American military history. Detailed biographies of Nathan Hale, Douglas MacArthur, Mary Hallaren, others. Chronologies of engagements, more. Introduction. Addenda. 1,033 entries in alphabetical order. xi + 548pp. 6½ × 9¼. (Available in U.S. only)
24758-9 Pa. $11.95

LIFE IN ANCIENT EGYPT, Adolf Erman. Detailed older account, with much not in more recent books: domestic life, religion, magic, medicine, commerce, and whatever else needed for complete picture. Many illustrations. 597pp. 5⅜ × 8½.
22632-8 Pa. $8.95

HISTORIC COSTUME IN PICTURES, Braun & Schneider. Over 1,450 costumed figures shown, covering a wide variety of peoples: kings, emperors, nobles, priests, servants, soldiers, scholars, townsfolk, peasants, merchants, courtiers, cavaliers, and more. 256pp. 8⅜ × 11¼. 23150-X Pa. $7.95

THE NOTEBOOKS OF LEONARDO DA VINCI, edited by J. P. Richter. Extracts from manuscripts reveal great genius; on painting, sculpture, anatomy, sciences, geography, etc. Both Italian and English. 186 ms. pages reproduced, plus 500 additional drawings, including studies for *Last Supper, Sforza* monument, etc. 860pp. 7⅞ × 10¾. (Available in U.S. only) 22572-0, 22573-9 Pa., Two-vol. set $25.90

THE ART NOUVEAU STYLE BOOK OF ALPHONSE MUCHA: All 72 Plates from "Documents Decoratifs" in Original Color, Alphonse Mucha. Rare copyright-free design portfolio by high priest of Art Nouveau. Jewelry, wallpaper, stained glass, furniture, figure studies, plant and animal motifs, etc. Only complete one-volume edition. 80pp. 9⅜ × 12¼. 24044-4 Pa. $8.95

ANIMALS: 1,419 COPYRIGHT-FREE ILLUSTRATIONS OF MAMMALS, BIRDS, FISH, INSECTS, ETC., edited by Jim Harter. Clear wood engravings present, in extremely lifelike poses, over 1,000 species of animals. One of the most extensive pictorial sourcebooks of its kind. Captions. Index. 284pp. 9 × 12. 23766-4 Pa. $9.95

OBELISTS FLY HIGH, C. Daly King. Masterpiece of American detective fiction, long out of print, involves murder on a 1935 transcontinental flight—"a very thrilling story"—NY Times. Unabridged and unaltered republication of the edition published by William Collins Sons & Co. Ltd., London, 1935. 288pp. 5⅜ × 8½. (Available in U.S. only) 25036-9 Pa. $4.95

VICTORIAN AND EDWARDIAN FASHION: A Photographic Survey, Alison Gernsheim. First fashion history completely illustrated by contemporary photographs. Full text plus 235 photos, 1840–1914, in which many celebrities appear. 240pp. 6½ × 9¼. 24205-6 Pa. $6.00

THE ART OF THE FRENCH ILLUSTRATED BOOK, 1700–1914, Gordon N. Ray. Over 630 superb book illustrations by Fragonard, Delacroix, Daumier, Doré, Grandville, Manet, Mucha, Steinlen, Toulouse-Lautrec and many others. Preface. Introduction. 633 halftones. Indices of artists, authors & titles, binders and provenances. Appendices. Bibliography. 608pp. 8⅜ × 11¼. 25086-5 Pa. $24.95

THE WONDERFUL WIZARD OF OZ, L. Frank Baum. Facsimile in full color of America's finest children's classic. 143 illustrations by W. W. Denslow. 267pp. 5⅜ × 8½. 20691-2 Pa. $5.95

FRONTIERS OF MODERN PHYSICS: New Perspectives on Cosmology, Relativity, Black Holes and Extraterrestrial Intelligence, Tony Rothman, et al. For the intelligent layman. Subjects include: cosmological models of the universe; black holes; the neutrino; the search for extraterrestrial intelligence. Introduction. 46 black-and-white illustrations. 192pp. 5⅜ × 8½. 24587-X Pa. $6.95

THE FRIENDLY STARS, Martha Evans Martin & Donald Howard Menzel. Classic text marshalls the stars together in an engaging, non-technical survey, presenting them as sources of beauty in night sky. 23 illustrations. Foreword. 2 star charts. Index. 147pp. 5⅜ × 8½. 21099-5 Pa. $3.50

FADS AND FALLACIES IN THE NAME OF SCIENCE, Martin Gardner. Fair, witty appraisal of cranks, quacks, and quackeries of science and pseudoscience: hollow earth, Velikovsky, orgone energy, Dianetics, flying saucers, Bridey Murphy, food and medical fads, etc. Revised, expanded In the Name of Science. "A very able and even-tempered presentation."—The New Yorker. 363pp. 5⅜ × 8. 20394-8 Pa. $5.95

ANCIENT EGYPT: ITS CULTURE AND HISTORY, J. E Manchip White. From pre-dynastics through Ptolemies: society, history, political structure, religion, daily life, literature, cultural heritage. 48 plates. 217pp. 5⅜ × 8½. 22548-8 Pa. $4.95

SIR HARRY HOTSPUR OF HUMBLETHWAITE, Anthony Trollope. Incisive, unconventional psychological study of a conflict between a wealthy baronet, his idealistic daughter, and their scapegrace cousin. The 1870 novel in its first inexpensive edition in years. 250pp. 5⅜ × 8½.   24953-0 Pa. $4.95

LASERS AND HOLOGRAPHY, Winston E. Kock. Sound introduction to burgeoning field, expanded (1981) for second edition. Wave patterns, coherence, lasers, diffraction, zone plates, properties of holograms, recent advances. 84 illustrations. 160pp. 5⅜ × 8¼. (Except in United Kingdom)   24041-X Pa. $3.50

INTRODUCTION TO ARTIFICIAL INTELLIGENCE: SECOND, EN-LARGED EDITION, Philip C. Jackson, Jr. Comprehensive survey of artificial intelligence—the study of how machines (computers) can be made to act intelligently. Includes introductory and advanced material. Extensive notes updating the main text. 132 black-and-white illustrations. 512pp. 5⅜ × 8½.   24864-X Pa. $8.95

HISTORY OF INDIAN AND INDONESIAN ART, Ananda K. Coomaraswamy. Over 400 illustrations illuminate classic study of Indian art from earliest Harappa finds to early 20th century. Provides philosophical, religious and social insights. 304pp. 6⅜ × 9⅜.   25005-9 Pa. $8.95

THE GOLEM, Gustav Meyrink. Most famous supernatural novel in modern European literature, set in Ghetto of Old Prague around 1890. Compelling story of mystical experiences, strange transformations, profound terror. 13 black-and-white illustrations. 224pp. 5⅜ × 8½. (Available in U.S. only)   25025-3 Pa. $5.95

ARMADALE, Wilkie Collins. Third great mystery novel by the author of *The Woman in White* and *The Moonstone*. Original magazine version with 40 illustrations. 597pp. 5⅜ × 8½.   23429-0 Pa. $7.95

PICTORIAL ENCYCLOPEDIA OF HISTORIC ARCHITECTURAL PLANS, DETAILS AND ELEMENTS: With 1,880 Line Drawings of Arches, Domes, Doorways, Facades, Gables, Windows, etc., John Theodore Haneman. Sourcebook of inspiration for architects, designers, others. Bibliography. Captions. 141pp. 9 × 12.   24605-1 Pa. $6.95

BENCHLEY LOST AND FOUND, Robert Benchley. Finest humor from early 30's, about pet peeves, child psychologists, post office and others. Mostly unavailable elsewhere. 73 illustrations by Peter Arno and others. 183pp. 5⅜ × 8½.
                    22410-4 Pa. $3.95

ERTÉ GRAPHICS, Erté. Collection of striking color graphics: *Seasons, Alphabet, Numerals, Aces* and *Precious Stones.* 50 plates, including 4 on covers. 48pp. 9⅜ × 12¼.   23580-7 Pa. $6.95

THE JOURNAL OF HENRY D. THOREAU, edited by Bradford Torrey, F. H. Allen. Complete reprinting of 14 volumes, 1837–61, over two million words; the sourcebooks for *Walden,* etc. Definitive. All original sketches, plus 75 photographs. 1,804pp. 8½ × 12¼.   20312-3, 20313-1 Cloth., Two-vol. set $80.00

CASTLES: THEIR CONSTRUCTION AND HISTORY, Sidney Toy. Traces castle development from ancient roots. Nearly 200 photographs and drawings illustrate moats, keeps, baileys, many other features. Caernarvon, Dover Castles, Hadrian's Wall, Tower of London, dozens more. 256pp. 5⅜ × 8¼.
                    24898-4 Pa. $5.95

AMERICAN CLIPPER SHIPS: 1833–1858, Octavius T. Howe & Frederick C. Matthews. Fully-illustrated, encyclopedic review of 352 clipper ships from the period of America's greatest maritime supremacy. Introduction. 109 halftones. 5 black-and-white line illustrations. Index. Total of 928pp. 5⅜ × 8½.
25115-2, 25116-0 Pa., Two-vol. set $17.90

TOWARDS A NEW ARCHITECTURE, Le Corbusier. Pioneering manifesto by great architect, near legendary founder of "International School." Technical and aesthetic theories, views on industry, economics, relation of form to function, "mass-production spirit," much more. Profusely illustrated. Unabridged translation of 13th French edition. Introduction by Frederick Etchells. 320pp. 6⅛ × 9¼. (Available in U.S. only)
25023-7 Pa. $8.95

THE BOOK OF KELLS, edited by Blanche Cirker. Inexpensive collection of 32 full-color, full-page plates from the greatest illuminated manuscript of the Middle Ages, painstakingly reproduced from rare facsimile edition. Publisher's Note. Captions. 32pp. 9⅜ × 12¼.
24345-1 Pa. $4.95

BEST SCIENCE FICTION STORIES OF H. G. WELLS, H. G. Wells. Full novel *The Invisible Man*, plus 17 short stories: "The Crystal Egg," "Aepyornis Island," "The Strange Orchid," etc. 303pp. 5⅜ × 8½. (Available in U.S. only)
21531-8 Pa. $4.95

AMERICAN SAILING SHIPS: Their Plans and History, Charles G. Davis. Photos, construction details of schooners, frigates, clippers, other sailcraft of 18th to early 20th centuries—plus entertaining discourse on design, rigging, nautical lore, much more. 137 black-and-white illustrations. 240pp. 6⅛ × 9¼.
24658-2 Pa. $5.95

ENTERTAINING MATHEMATICAL PUZZLES, Martin Gardner. Selection of author's favorite conundrums involving arithmetic, money, speed, etc., with lively commentary. Complete solutions. 112pp. 5⅜ × 8½.
25211-6 Pa. $2.95

THE WILL TO BELIEVE, HUMAN IMMORTALITY, William James. Two books bound together. Effect of irrational on logical, and arguments for human immortality. 402pp. 5⅜ × 8½.
20291-7 Pa. $7.50

THE HAUNTED MONASTERY and THE CHINESE MAZE MURDERS, Robert Van Gulik. 2 full novels by Van Gulik continue adventures of Judge Dee and his companions. An evil Taoist monastery, seemingly supernatural events; overgrown topiary maze that hides strange crimes. Set in 7th-century China. 27 illustrations. 328pp. 5⅜ × 8½.
23502-5 Pa. $5.95

CELEBRATED CASES OF JUDGE DEE (DEE GOONG AN), translated by Robert Van Gulik. Authentic 18th-century Chinese detective novel; Dee and associates solve three interlocked cases. Led to Van Gulik's own stories with same characters. Extensive introduction. 9 illustrations. 237pp. 5⅜ × 8½.
23337-5 Pa. $4.95

Prices subject to change without notice.
Available at your book dealer or write for free catalog to Dept. GI, Dover Publications, Inc., 31 East 2nd St., Mineola, N.Y. 11501. Dover publishes more than 175 books each year on science, elementary and advanced mathematics, biology, music, art, literary history, social sciences and other areas.